Embracing Hope in the Midst of
Stormy Times

Embracing Hope in the Midst of Stormy Times

Heather D. Wright

Colorful Spirit Publishing

Boone, North Carolina

Contents

Title   ix

Copyright Information   x

Dedication   xi

Introduction   1

1. Chapter 1 - A Lost Heart in Search of Direction   3

2. Chapter 2 - A New Year's Prayer   7

3. Chapter 3 - A Trip Through the Mountains and Valleys of Life   12

4. Chapter 4 - Emotional Bankruptcy   17

5. Chapter 5 - Falling Deeper and Deeper   22

6. Chapter 6 - Following the Heart Outside the Box of Hopeless Expectations   27

7. Chapter 7 - Hanging on to Hope Through Simple Prayers   31

8. Chapter 8 - My Broken-winged Friend Called Hope   35

9.   Chapter 9 – Pandora's Box   39

10. Chapter 10 – Pieces from a Weary Soul's   43
     Heart

11. Chapter 11 – Regrets that Led to a Brighter   47
     Tomorrow

12. Chapter 12 – The Cage and a Kind Spirit   51
     Guide

13. Chapter 13 – The Caged Butterfly on the   55
     Path to Freedom

14. Chapter 14 – The Day Hope Took the Last   60
     Guilt Trip

15. Chapter 15 – The Desperate But Healing   64
     Heart

16. Chapter 16 – The Echo of a Broken Soul   69
     Searching for Direction

17. Chapter 17 – The Flower Garden of   73
     Tranquility

18. Chapter 18 – The Forgiving Tree   77

19. Chapter 19 – The Game of Addiction   82

20. Chapter 20 – The Heart That Cried for Help   86

21. Chapter 21 – The Heartbreak That Never   90
     Seems to End

22. Chapter 22 – The Magician With The   94
     Deceptive Heart

23. Chapter 23 – The Pieces of the Puzzle Called   98
     Life

24. Chapter 24 - The Raging River of Fear   *102*

25. Chapter 25 - The Shadows of an Exhausted   *106*
Spirit

26. Chapter 26 - The Teddy Bear in the Toybox   *110*
of Lost Dreams

27. Chapter 27 - Trapped   *114*

28. Chapter 28 - Waking Up Tired   *117*

29. Chapter 29 - Mr. High Hopes and Wolves in   *120*
Sheep's Clothing

30. Chapter 30 - The Honest Apple   *124*

31. Chapter 31 - The Heartfelt Connection   *128*

32. Chapter 32 - The Angel and the Streets of   *132*
Gold

33. Chapter 33 - Walking in the Shadows   *136*

34. Chapter 34 - Spiritual Protection in the   *140*
Midst of a Seagull Collection

35. Chapter 35 - The Rearview Mirror and the   *144*
Destined Road

36. Chapter 36 - Games Energy Vampires Play   *148*

37. Chapter 37 - Confusion and Disillusion that   *152*
Led to Something Soothing

38. Chapter 38 - The Magic Drink Called Peace   *156*
of Mind

39. Chapter 39 - The Disease Called Emotional   *160*
Fatigue

40. Chapter 40 – The Suitcase Solution   164

41. Chapter 41 – Sleepwalking Through Time   168

42. Chapter 42 – Karmic Justice and All Those   172
    Pesky Flies

43. Chapter 43 – The Secret to Happiness   176

44. Chapter 44 – The Brevity of Life   180

45. Chapter 45 – The Test of Time   184

46. Chapter 46 – Swimming Upstream In the   188
    Midst of Hopeful Dreams

47. Chapter 47 – The Imprisoned Castle and the   192
    Butterfly of Freedom

48. Chapter 48 – The Mystery Mailbox   196

49. Chapter 49 – The Desperate Bridge Called   200
    Suicide

50. Chapter 50 – True Destiny   204

    Afterword   207
    About the Author   209

Title

*EMBRACING HOPE IN THE MIDST OF STORMY
TIMES*

BY HEATHER D. WRIGHT

COURTESY OF COLORFUL SPIRIT PUBLISHING

Copyright Information

Dedication

This book is dedicated to my Aunt Donna whose hard battle with cancer inspired me to never give up no matter how tough things may get. Thank you for being a true inspiration and angel to all who loved you.

Introduction

For most of my life, I was always taught that love is the most important thing of all to embrace, and even though it is truly important to feel and to experience, I have come to see that hope is really what keeps us anchored through all the storms of this life. It would be nice if life was full of one success right after the other, but the truth is that the hard times are what truly helps us become stronger when it seems all the odds of life are against us.

If there is one word that has become the heart and soul of who I truly am, it is the word struggle as it is through my own struggles I have truly learned what survival in the midst of the storm is all about. When I think about struggle, in fact, I always think about hope as well because they both are connected as when we struggle we strive to find the hope for better days and a better life. So many people want to reach the good things in life, but what I have realized, and what so many others come to see as well, is that we often have to endure some difficult battles in order to appreciate all the many beautiful gifts God has in store for us.

In this book, *Embracing Hope in the Midst of Stormy Times*, my desire is that every commentary and poetic piece uplifts your heart and soul to help you understand that suffering leads to a new way of life for all of us. I believe everything happens for a reason, and even when many things happen that I do not understand, I have learned to just keep my hopes held high and know eventually everything has a way of working out for the best.

Chapter 1 - A Lost Heart in Search of Direction

Ever feel so confused and lost as if nobody truly understands you? Ever feel like you wish you could escape from your normal existence into a time and place where life does not seem as difficult? Ever hope that one day someone may come along with a fresh outlook on life to help you rise above your struggles and feel good about yourself when the whole world seems against you?

If you can answer affirmatively to all of these questions, than you, like so many of us, have suffered from a lost heart searching for direction and more meaning in your life. No matter how good and bad life may become, we all need to know there is at least one true love or one true friend who totally understands us when the rest of the world is trying to break us down.

The following poem, "A Lost Heart in Search of Direction", is all about finding meaning in life and knowing that when all hope is lost, that God often sends a true friend who will encourage us always.

A Lost Heart in Search of Direction

Once upon a time there lived a lost heart
In search of a much needed direction
Over the course of time it had loved and
Lost so much and endured countless rejection

This lost heart tried and tried to find
A way out of the jungle of its distress
Every night it prayed to God hoping
He would somehow give it some much needed rest

The lost heart spent many years hoping to
Connect with one soul who would be a true friend
Yet all it found were some dishonest people
Whose deceptive charms led to misery once again

No matter where it looked or
How hard it tried to survive
The lost heart never seemed to make it
Through the night without a good, long cry

As the months and years rolled by it seemed
The lost heart just found itself trapped in despair
It often looked within and questioned if there
Was anyone out there who truly cared

Sometimes the lost heart never did think it would
Ever find someone to keep its heart beating
Throughout the past it discovered false charmers
Who got their way by always cheating

The lost heart was often so frustrated
To always run into so many crazy setbacks
All it really wanted was a true friend it could
Love and trust to help it get back on track

After all the false hopes and attempts
To find one honest spirit who it could really trust
It just became ready to give up
And escape its forever bad luck

Then one day when the lost heart was ready
To give up on finding someone it could love
A magical soul walked into its presence
With loving eyes sent straight from the Heavens above

This wonderful spirit just smiled brightly
At the lost heart as if to say I know where you have been
It spoke a language without words as if to tell
The lost heart I will be your most trusted friend

The lost heart could feel its pain melt away
As this dynamic soul embraced it with its bright eyes
In a moment of brief connection the lost heart
Found a true friend and a love that would never die

As the weeks passed by the heart felt it
No longer was as lost as it once was in the past
Its misery was now replaced by the love of an
Honest, spiritual soul destined to last

The heart learned that his new, special friend
Was sent from God so it would never be alone
Whether together or apart the two connected
So strongly they agreed to not let each other go

During all the good and bad moments that the heart
And its treasured friend went through
They were linked by a legacy of spiritual friendship
And a love that would remain forever true

Chapter 2 - A New Year's Prayer

I have always loved New Year's Eve. For some people, New Year's Eve is the time for parties and having a blast. For me it has always been a time of reflection when I think back to all the times in my past where I tried too hard or should have tried much less. New Year's Eve is a time for me when I really look back for a moment in time and wonder if what I did or what I said truly made a difference in the lives of those whose paths crossed mine.

Like so many people, I have made my fair share of New Year's Resolutions, and I have also failed miserably at making so many of them happen. However, I learned not too long ago that the best things we can hope for when a new year begins is to just say a simple prayer asking God to grant you the desires of your heart and protect the ones you love along the way. I have discovered through my own journeys in this life that the more I hold on to the promises of God, the more He holds on to me. All of my prayers have been answered, and in some ways, I may have not always gotten the answer I had hoped for, but I certainly got the one God intended for me to have.

The following poem, "A New Year's Prayer", is my personal prayer of hope for all of you that in searching for your path in this life that you truly find the keys to your soul's growth.

A New Year's Prayer

I was lying in bed wondering
What happened to the time
I kept thinking somehow this year flew past
Too quickly with an interesting new rhyme

When I looked back over all that
This past year had brought
Somehow I could feel I had grown more spiritually
And learned from the lessons I had been taught

I started thinking back over every mistake
I had made that made me sad
Then I thought about all my careless setbacks
And the people who had made me mad

Even though I could never quite understand
Why I was still struggling on the inside

I could remember having to pretend to be happy
Even when I could barely make it on the outside

There were times over the past year
I felt so down and dreary
Then there were other moments I had worked so hard
That I just felt defeated and weary

I thought about the family I spent time with
Who helped me feel I would always belong
Then I remembered all the old and new friends
Who greeted my path with both familiar and new songs

I could not understand why another year
Had finally come to an end
Yet I decided to say a prayer to God that the new year
Would bring greater blessings like a good friend

I prayed and asked God to help me to
Remain always in His care
I asked Him to give me forever peace
And a heart of love that would always be there

I asked Him to give me strength to endure times
When I felt I could not go on
Then I prayed for the courage to keep helping others
Learn from life during its sad songs

I then prayed that my family
Would always be protected

Then I asked that my friends would learn from life's tragedies
And have bad karma completely rejected

I thought about my career and prayed God
Would help me continue to teach and write with joy
Then I asked God to give me constant words
That build up others and help them overcome turmoil

I thought about the path of love and how it had always been
One that is so hard for so many to find
But I prayed God would help the hearts of many
To embrace a spiritual love that lasts the test of time

As another year ends
And a new year begins
I prayed that God would help me never lose sight
That true happiness always comes from within

As another year became a chapter
In the history of my much blessed life
I silently closed my prayer asking God
To surround my heart and soul with spiritual love and light

Life is so short and none of us ever know
When one year could be our last
I have been wounded from bad choices
And haunted from memories from my past

Looking back I can see that everything I endured
Was for a much spiritual reason

I just looked up and thanked God that the time
Had come to make a fresh start in a brand new season

Chapter 3 - A Trip Through the Mountains and Valleys of Life

Life is all about the highs and lows we experience. Everyday and through every season we take trips. Some trips are full of great joy and have the ability to transform our lives in the most profound ways possible. Some trips are full of valleys where the pain is hard to endure, but we must go through the struggles in order to learn the lessons God wants us to know.

When it comes to journeys, so many of us would like to live on that mountain where everything seems to fall into place for us. However, the reality is that we are meant to grow and change, and often when life is wonderful, we get complacent thinking we can stay in our comfort zone and just be happy. Even though that feeling is great, we do not learn as much on the mountain. The moment we fall into the valleys of our lives is the very moment when God teaches us that true change and growth comes when we are at the lowest, the times when we learn to let go and let God take control of our lives.

As you read the following poem, "A Trip Through the Mountains and Valleys of Life", you will find one soul's journey through his own ups and downs and the good things learned along the way.

A Trip Through the Mountains and Valleys of Life

Once upon a time in the midst of
A spiritual destiny created long ago
God said get ready to go on a trip where your soul
Will one day grow strong and forever bold

Confused and unsure of how my
Journey in this life might be
I just decided to keep the faith
No matter what my life threw at me

There were times my journey took me to
Great mountains where the view was quite breathless

No matter what anybody said to me
I could face the edge without fear or feeling so restless

Sometimes I even felt I could take a few risks
And jump high right into the sky
I could soar with the birds in the air
Without a care in the world or a reason to ask why

Then there were times I could not fly
With the graceful birds that became my trusted friends
I could not fly as high as them and found myself
Falling fast into a valley crushing my spirit within

In the valley of craziness I struggled to find some way
Out of a place that made me feel so sick
But within the depth of my heart and soul
I knew I had fallen victim to misfortune's clever tricks

During the days in the valley I asked God
To somehow set me free from all my pain
After sleeping in a tunnel of despair
I found myself greeting the sun after a period of cold, hard rain

The path upon which I walked now had
A fresh, new glow full of charm and grace
Although I once was on top of the world
My hard lessons were paving for me a better way

I found an exciting new path that
I felt God wanted for me to travel

He whispered to just hang tough cause
I would face times where I would feel completely rattled

Thinking I could handle any setback
That tried to trouble my soul
I just made things worse when God cried
When will you learn to trust me to never let you go

I let my pride get in the way
Of every step I took
It was like I was determined to walk my own way
And write the words to my most desperate book

Even when everything seemed to be
Happening according to my own plan
God just cried out you are heading right into the valley
Where you will soon mess up again

Thinking I was invincible and that nothing
Could really tear my world apart
God said you can't have everything the way you think
It should be and ignore your own heart

I just kept climbing my own mountain
Determined to do everything my own way
The next thing I knew I lost my balance falling
Right into the valley again feeling further lost and afraid

With tears of frustration I prayed and asked God
When the struggles would ever stop

He just whispered when hard times come
You don't learn lessons needed on the mountain top

I was angry and demanding God put me back
On top of the world where everything seemed great
God just whispered learn from your mistakes
In the valley and you will grow strong again one day

I spent many long days and nights in this valley
That I never thought would ever let me breathe
Yet somehow during all my nightmares
A pleasant dream or two would bring me some peace

I slowly but surely through a new found faith
Was able to crawl out of the pit of my despair
God said just keep holding my hand
And I will take you to a new mountain with serene air

Every now and then I reflect back on the journey
I was meant to take for my own path
Although the mountain top experiences were fun
It was in the valley I learned not to look back

Now every time and again when I feel
On top of the mountain of great luck
God keeps holding my hand when I'm in the valleys
With much love and a spirit that never gives up

Chapter 4 - Emotional Bankruptcy

When everything in life is going well, it is easy to assume that there will not be any challenges to come our way. We start thinking that nothing can go wrong, and we can handle anything life throws at us. Over time the reality is that none of us escape hard times. Some people have a tough time knowing how to endure struggles in life. In fact, we can easily become so overwhelmed that it feels as if nothing can help us overcome the depression and sadness we feel.

After enduring so many tough battles, it is often easy to become emotionally drained to the point it feels we cannot make it from one day to the next. When life gets tough, sometimes our emotions can get the better of us and leave us feeling as if we have nothing left to give. We begin to start losing our hope in a better way of life.

The following poem, "Emotional Bankruptcy", focuses on the story of a hummingbird who has been wounded by false promises and betrayals in his life. This poem focuses on the bird's journey back into his past to try and make sense of the struggles he endured and to not let present defeats bring him down. Even though he feels emotionally drained, he continues to keep the faith knowing that better days lie ahead.

Emotional Bankruptcy

There once was a hummingbird with an almost
Broken wing that still desperately wanted to fly
Yet somehow it had been haunted by its past of
Lost connections and unanswered whys

In the midst of its pain the hummingbird thought
Maybe it could flap its wings and fly away
Yet it could not escape all the years it had been
Treated badly and left in the cold on long, hard days

It managed to fly a little ways back on a path
That to most did not make sense

Yet in its mind the hummingbird knew it had to fly
Back in time to recover from so many false promises

In its travel back through time the hummingbird
Caught a glimpse of when it gave all it had to give
Then before it could fly further back it realized
That even when hurt it somehow had to forgive

As the hummingbird flew a little further back
On a path that was full of such pain
It was shown a time in its life when all of its goodness
And kind spirit was put to complete shame

Somehow the hummingbird felt the journey
Back on this path might be too hard to bear
Yet in its weary heart it somehow wanted to see
If there was anyone back then who really cared

In times of tough trials
And complete desperation
The hummingbird kept going back in time
To find out why it felt lost in a world of rejection

On its journey the hummingbird was not
Really sure what else it was meant to see
Yet with what small breath it had it just wanted
To find a way out of all its misery

Even though most of God's creatures would
Not want to be reminded of hard times past

The little hummingbird knew that it had to
Endure trouble so the good times would come back

As it flew in despair further down a path where
The darkness seemed to consume its soul
It just flapped its wings as a cry of hope that
God would give it the strength to never let go

As time passed the little hummingbird was shown
So many moments where its heart had been broken
Then it could hear echoes of hurtful words that
Would have been best if they had been left unspoken

In the dark of night the hummingbird knew
That during all the times it felt so lost and confused
There had to be a time when true peace would come
And give relief to the times it felt so used

Through its journey back in time the hummingbird
Knew it had to remain strong
As hard as it was to fly with an almost broken wing
It knew that it had to endure certain sad songs

After a tough trip down on a path that
Was not an easy one to endure
The hummingbird managed to find a light to
A new path where it felt strong again and reassured

As it reached a meadow full of bright flowers
And lots of sun to guide its way

The little hummingbird noticed its almost broken wing
Had been healed over time because of its faith

With joy in its heart the hummingbird had discovered
A new life full of peace from the Heavens above
The emotional bankruptcy that once wounded its soul
Was now a treasure of hope and spiritual love

Chapter 5 - Falling Deeper and Deeper

Life is all about making mistakes and learning that everything we choose to do is meant to help us grow on our spiritual path. I have felt many times that I could not survive many of the setbacks I have faced in my own life. In fact, there have been so many times that I thought I was lost in a world of broken dreams and misguided promises. Every time I have felt this way it seems it is all I can do to face a brand new day. We all have moments in each of our lives where it feels that the obstacles we face are enough to break us down so much to the point we feel just like giving up.

The following poem, "Falling Deeper and Deeper", is a reflection of one soul's struggles in life and his challenge to remain strong to endure and overcome life's trials and tribulations. It is also a poem of hope and knowing that often God uses the power of love to set us free from our broken hearts so we know we are truly loved and never alone.

No matter how up or down you may feel in your own life, just remember things do get better and that love has the power to heal us when we need it most.

Falling Deeper and Deeper

I was falling deeper and deeper into
A part of myself I was too scared to know
It was like all the dark forces around were determined
To keep me down and never let me go

I was falling deeper and deeper into a
Place that I barely could understand
All I wanted was to ask God to free me from
All my fears and walk with me hand in hand

I was falling deeper and deeper into
A world where time did not stand still
It was like I had been sent on a journey to
Revisit all my hurts that I hoped some day would heal

I was falling deeper and deeper into
A world where I just wanted to escape

All I really hoped for was a place to be
At peace and all my troubles would fall away

I was falling deeper and deeper into
A world that I did not really trust
All the voices inside my mind tried to get me
To listen to them when I was feeling so out of luck

I was falling deeper and deeper into a cage of despair
That made me feel I was not so great
No matter how much I tried to believe in myself
I always felt like I was misfortune's mistake

I was falling deeper and deeper into an abyss
Of lost hope that just seemed to bring me down
No matter how much I wanted to keep my forever smile
There was always a frown to be found

I was falling deeper and deeper into a
Magical destiny I so wanted to embrace
Yet many jealous souls wanted to steal my joy
And leave me feeling like an utter disgrace

I was falling deeper and deeper into
A dream that I so wanted to reach
Yet I found myself just falling so fast into
Darkness I lost my ability to really teach

I was falling deeper and deeper into a foreign land
Where everyone else had so much

Yet I remained the poor soul barely making ends meet
And lacking money's golden touch

I was falling deeper and deeper into an endless fatigue
That I so desperately tried to stop
Yet no matter how much I wanted to try harder
I felt my weary spirit giving up quite a lot

I was falling deeper and deeper into a maze
Of no direction and I could not find my way
All I could do was keep praying that God
Would somehow show me a better way

I was falling deeper and deeper into past lives
Where I had loved and lost so many times
Yet I felt my soulmate's love breathing new energy
Into my spirit with a new vision and rhyme

I was falling deeper and deeper into the heart
Of a kindred spirit that I adored beyond measure
No matter how much others tried to keep us apart
Our hearts and souls would always be together

I was falling deeper and deeper into the hands
Of love because God wanted to set me free
He just whispered look into the eyes of the one
I sent to love you so unconditionally

I was falling deeper and deeper into a new time
And place where a spiritual connection had begun

Through all the times I find myself falling deeper
I hope to fall into the arms of my soul's true love

Chapter 6 - Following the Heart Outside the Box of Hopeless Expectations

Thinking outside the box is so important. In a world where everyone often expects us to conform to certain standards of how we should think and feel, it is good to venture out on our own path of self-discovery. I have always been one to walk an unconventional path at times. Following the crowd has never been my desire, and every time I did so to please other people, I ended up feeling miserable in the process. Therefore, I have learned that it is best to be true to yourself and follow your own heart no matter what anyone else thinks or says.

The following poem, "Following the Heart Outside the Box of Hopeless Expectations", paints a true picture of one person's desire to follow his own path and to make his own choices based on what he desires rather than what he thinks will make others happy. The individual in this poem is in search of a better way of living and wants so much to be true to his heart and make decisions that will bring him the true happiness his soul seeks.

Sometimes we all have to walk a different path to find true happiness even if it means acting and thinking for ourselves to find true peace of mind.

Following the Heart Outside the Box of Hopeless Expectations

I was following my heart to a place
Where I was not sure I should go
Yet my soul kept telling me this is the one
You really love and should never feel low

I knew I could stay right where I was
And please everyone around me just to make them smile
But I could tell I would always be the one
Feeling frustrated and lost and far from worthwhile

Somehow I was not sure
How much more I could take

At some point I could stay just in a world of security
But all the while my heart would break

For me the road to love has not always been
A conventional one for me to embrace
There were times life seemed too hard while
I continued to feel like a complete disgrace

I wondered how much further I could take this path
To find the answers I so needed to know
No matter how hard I try to be logical my heart said
You love someone too much to ever let go

Other people thought they knew the answers
To find the one who was just right for me
Yet I realized that all they knew was how
To fit me into their box of expectations so willingly

I thought and thought about how many times
I tried to love others on the conventional path
I remembered having many heartbreaks
As memories came from all my times of hopelessly looking
back

I looked inside my heart and saw just how much
It wanted to color outside the lines of conformity
All I needed was to begin again and give myself
A fresh start to love with the right spiritual remedy

I fell in love with a spiritual soul a lot like mine

In a way that nobody could ever understand
When everyone else pretended to be happy
His eyes could warm my broken spirit like nobody else can

Some days I wonder if I will ever really be a part
Of a world where it is ok to love who you feel
Maybe I walk an unconventional path but
God gave me the most spiritual love that is strong and real

There are long days where my heart connects
With a spiritual lover unlike anything I've ever known
When others are trying to break me down
I feel his soul takes me back to a more loving home

In a dream I can follow my heart where I can be
With the one I love without anyone keeping us apart
The troubles in the outside world hurt us
But with this love I know it can heal my wounded heart

I have realized through every journey I have traveled
This love has been there with me many times
Together we share a spiritual destiny that keeps us
United in love with the most melodious rhyme

Through all my ups and downs I have learned
To follow my heart no matter how hard it may be
I keep the faith the miracle of a spiritual love
God has given will fulfill my destiny

Chapter 7 - Hanging on to Hope Through Simple Prayers

Throughout my entire life I have always believed in the power of prayer. God has always been the one I know I can trust to be there for me no matter now many times I have wanted to fall apart. Over the course of my life, I have prayed so many prayers, some of which were answered just like I wanted them to be and others not quite like I thought they would be. Despite the answers I may have gotten and despite the countless questions I asked, God always had the right answers for each of my dilemmas. The one thing I have learned most about the power of prayer is not to ever lose hope.

The following poem, "Hanging on to Hope Through Simple Prayers", is my own personal reflection of all the times I have cried out to God to help me and all the times He faithfully answered me. As I have learned, never lose sight of prayer and always have great hope that with every word you utter to God, just know He is always listening and will take care of your needs in the best ways possible.

Life is not easy for any of us, but when we pray I have learned to hope that divine intervention is always just around the corner.

Hanging on to Hope Through Simple Prayers

I got down on my knees and
Asked God to give me a break
God said I know you are tired of feeling uneasy
And in need of a fresh new day

I prayed aloud and asked God to help me
Find a way out of this maze of a life
God said it is through the challenging times
You gain strength without the need to always ask why

I prayed and told God I was frustrated that
I could never seem to catch a break no matter what

God just smiled at me and whispered
You know I send you tests because I love you a lot

I prayed for a time when I could just smile
Without having to worry when the other shoe would drop
God wrapped His loving arms around me saying
Sometimes we get lost before we come out on top

I prayed for a moment in time when I could run away
As far as my dreams would allow
God sent me a warm feeling within to encourage me
One day life would get easier somehow

I prayed for one of those coastal water vacations
That somehow would never end
God just smiled at me and let me know sometimes
You have to keep working hard in order to win

I prayed for a time when I could find
A way to quit swimming upstream
God whispered into my heart keep the faith
Because life is not always what it may seem

I prayed and asked God to help me find
Some way out of the box of crushed dreams and despair
God just kindly reminded me that it was through my losses
His love for me was always there

I prayed for the kind of freedom to fly as high in the air
Like a bird that's been set free from a cage

God just sent a gentle breeze to let me know
He will give me peace during any time of rage

I prayed and asked God why I had been
So blind to His plans for my journey
He said rest assured I will always be there to
Guide your path and give you a spirit that's discerning

I prayed and asked God to teach me how to use
A treasure chest of spiritual gifts just to feel safe
God smiled and said I wondered when you would
Let Me show how to endure life in a special way

Chapter 8 - My Broken-winged Friend
Called Hope

I have often found myself distraught time and time again wondering why it seemed I was constantly battling one problem right after the next. Many times I have fallen into a pit of total despair thinking that nobody really understood my pain or weary spirit. It has been in my darkest moments that I have felt God send a sign to me that things would get better and not to lose heart.

The following poem, "My Broken-winged Friend Called Hope", is inspired by my own true story as one day I found myself feeling so down in my spirit questioning why so many bad things had happened in my life.

In the middle of my own self-pity, I noticed a little sparrow struggling to fly as I was sitting outside a local restaurant.

Instead of continuing to think of my own problems, I decided to take care of this bird and somehow helped give it the strength to fly again. It was in this moment that I realized sometimes we help ourselves by helping someone or something else feel better.

My Broken-winged Friend Called Hope

I was feeling tired
And wondering what I should do
So I sat down at a cafe outside
A small town to have a drink or two

Much to my surprise I saw a brown sparrow bird
That was struggling to fly
The more it tried to flap its weary wings
The more I felt I should help him try

I knelt down to this sparrow to see
If I could help him heal
He barely could look me in the eye
But I could feel he needed a friend that was real

Somehow I was not sure what I should do
To help him get off the ground
Yet somewhere inside of his little heart
I could feel he wanted me to stick around

As the hot, summer sun made it hard
For the sparrow to barely stand up

I decided to give it some water to quench its thirsty soul
That was trying to remain tough

I wrapped my hand around the bird to try
And help him get back on his feet
Yet he seemed a little scared to stand too tall
For fear he was too weak from the draining heat

I rubbed his little head hoping I could comfort
His worried mind with a healing touch
Then I could feel his broken wing lift higher as if
He was trying to tell me he needed me so much

I felt maybe I should just stay right by his side to
Help him feel strong until he could fly away
But somehow he just needed the comforting presence
Of a true friend that would love him in every way

As I sat beside my friend I watched him stand up on his feet
And flap his wings to get my attention
In my deepest soul I was so glad I could help him
Find forever hope and constant protection

After just a few moments of caressing
His weak body with the touch of my hands
I felt an exchange of energy between us as if he finally
Found a friend in me that truly understands

Despite all the distractions around us
The sparrow and I stayed by each others' side

We became loving friends whose spirits were linked
With a loyal love that would never die

9

Chapter 9 - Pandora's Box

For my entire life I have always been intrigued by the notion of Pandora's Box. I had learned at an early age that this particular box is one that typically holds many unfortunate circumstances should it ever be opened. Even though I never have laid eyes on one of these actual boxes, I have certainly learned how easy it can be to stir up a hornet's nest when it's best to leave something alone.

If anything, I know that bad karma just generates more bad karma, and it is best to not be deceptive just to make a point. In the following poem, "Pandora's Box", the subject in this poem is totally intrigued by the seductive nature of a box that appears to be so beautiful yet its full of deceptive charms. However, the lesson from this poem is that just because something appears to be so beautiful on the inside does not mean it always is.

As I have told many family and friends over the course of time, if it seems too good to be true, it usually most certainly is. Always trust your instincts because some areas of life are meant for us to walk away from to keep us safe from destructive forces.

Pandora's Box

In the middle of the night
I had a most confusing dream
A bright, colorful box appeared that had
A most intriguing lure unlike anything I had ever seen

Tempted to open it I wondered what was
Inside this most fascinating gift
Maybe I just needed something more exciting
To give my heart some kind of spiritual uplift

I was not sure if I should take this leap of faith
And open something that could cause me harm
In the past I was often misled by
False promises and misguided charm

Back and forth in my mind I was curious
If I should open this mysterious box
My better instincts warned me it could bring
Lots of havoc to a heart about to stop

I walked around and around this box trying
To see if I knew the results of peeping inside

Yet my mind warned me once you take the leap
You cannot turn back this time

There were memories of times gone by and moments
That I knew I could never get back
Playing with the idea of opening this box
Could throw my whole world off track

I listened closely to try and understand
Exactly why this box had to appear
Just when I had found peace in my world an
Unexpected gift would leave me drowning in fear

After circling this box for hours trying to figure out
How I could ever let it go for good
I just stared at it longer wondering if maybe
I should run as far away and as best as I could

My heart was too weak to resist
The seductive nature of a box that had me feeling like a fool
My mind knew that this box was nothing but trouble
And I needed to keep my cool

This was the kind of pressure that I was
Not expected to really feel at all
I knew that what lay inside were false hopes and old hurts
Ready to take me for a fall

After what seemed forever toying with the idea
Of opening what I call Pandora's Box

I woke up from this dream knowing God
Brought Pandora's deceptive charms to a stop

Chapter 10 - Pieces from a Weary Soul's Heart

If there is anything I have come to know well in my life it would the heartbreak of betrayal. I have been hurt more times than I can count thinking someone I cared about felt the same way only to discover his or her level of caring was never on the same page as my own. I have truly come to understand that nothing hurts worse than caring deeply for another soul whose selfish interests outweigh the need to be empathetic and understanding.

At some point there will come a time in all of our lives when we all face the realization that there will be many people coming into our lives whose feelings and intentions are unfortunately not always on the same page as our own. Through the passage of time we all experience the pain of thinking something was truly real when in all actuality the person we thought we knew was only out to take advantage of our good heart. Despite the pain of this disappointment, I have discovered that there are some people that truly do care and sometimes we have to go through some tough times to be led to another who will love us no matter what.

The following poem, "Pieces of a Weary Soul's Heart", provides several examples of a soul who has faced one heartbreak after the other, yet despite the hurt of broken relationships over the course of time, finds true caring and solace in the heart of his or her true mate.

Pieces from a Weary Soul's Heart

A weary soul's heart had been broken
In pieces time and time again
It kept asking God when He would give it the strength
To not give up and be strong enough to win

He just kept telling it to take a look back
At all the places where its heart had stopped
Yet the weary soul was scared to go back for fear
The pain it brought would send it right over the top

There was a time when a piece of the weary
Soul's heart was lost by someone who put it down
This lover made it like it was not worthy and could
Always turn its smile into a constant frown

No matter how hard it tried to be good enough
For its lover it was always made to feel a fool
That was when a piece of the weary soul's heart
Was lost by someone whose love was never true

There was another time the weary soul fell fast
And hard that it felt like it had met its destiny
It was even offered a marriage proposal and
A promise for forever that became a sheer mockery

A piece of the weary soul's heart once again fell
Apart when the one it loved never loved it anyway
The weary soul was in despair because someone
It trusted broke its heart and just ran away

After two major pieces of the weary soul's heart
Had fallen away from its soul
It thought surely I can find someone to love me
Deeply who will never let me go

There came someone who seemed
Charming and full of great life
Yet all this soul wanted to do was have a great time
And put the weary soul through endless strife

Three major pieces of the weary soul's heart had
Fallen away from souls who were deceptive
It just felt like giving up on love because it realized
It was always way too receptive

Then came a promising soul that it thought
It would always be with forever
Yet another piece of the weary soul's heart fell away
When this lover was too scared for them to be together

All these pieces from a weary heart left
This poor soul feeling desperate and so alone
Then from a mystical place it connected with
A charming spirit whose heart became its new home

Through years and years of searching
For the right soul connection
The weary soul and its enchanting soul mate loved each other
Deeply for choosing love and all its great lessons

Chapter 11 - Regrets that Led to a Brighter Tomorrow

For so much of my life I have held on to many regrets. There have been times I regretted not being a better family member or a closer friend. There have been times I regretted not reaching out to a total stranger who maybe just needed to know that someone truly cared. I have spent many sleepless nights replaying certain situations over and over in my mind wondering if the outcome would have been different if I could have just said or done something much differently. As I have gotten older, I look back over the course of my life now and have come to realize that everything I have endured happened the way it did for a reason.

The following poem, "Regrets that Led to a Brighter Tomorrow", is all about not letting the power of regret suffocate the way we think and feel. It reflects the internal turmoil regrets bring into our mindset, and yet encourages us to learn from the cards we may have been dealt rather than holding on to something we cannot change.

It's human nature to have regrets, but our strength lies in learning that we cannot always control what someone else says or does, but we can certainly control how we react as that is truly the key to releasing the stress regrets can create.

Regrets that Led to a Brighter Tomorrow

I was lying in bed one night
So desperate to fall asleep
Yet the memories of all the regrets I had
Kept me awake feeling weary and weak

Somehow I kept hoping that I could find
A way to escape all the many regrets from my past
However I knew God wanted me to learn from
My mistakes and embrace a happier life that would last

My mind kept playing tricks telling me
I should have known better
But my heart told me I was just a lost soul
Looking for a way to keep my life together

Tears streamed down my face because
I felt all my wrong turns cost me so much time

I asked God when all my bad choices would disappear
So I could embrace the melody of life to a more joyous rhyme

Even though I was eager to find the answers
To bring peace to my much troubled soul
I knew all the times I made mistakes were hardships
I experienced to help my spirit to grow

Memories of times gone past with
Family and friends kept playing out in my head
I wished to revisit the good times but knew
I had to move on and face a new beginning instead

In the middle of what I felt was one
Of the toughest nights of my existence
I got up and looked into the mirror of change
With a renewed faith to overcome my present resistance

What once was a sad spirit turned into
A smile that lightened up my darkened room
It was not long before I caught a glimpse of
A sunrise promising a new life would begin for me soon

After taking a trip back through all the regrets
That tried to trap my heart in a world of sorrow
I realized these regrets were lessons to be learned
To give me courage to face a better tomorrow

I left my home after my dark night of the soul
Determined to not let anything bring me down

Everywhere nature's finest creations followed me
With great joy all through town

Some people look into the rear view mirror
Of their lives hoping to fix what they cant change
Now I know the importance of keeping the faith
Remains close to my heart keeping me fearlessly sane

Chapter 12 - The Cage and a Kind Spirit Guide

I have often felt drawn to other people who felt trapped in their lives by various circumstances that left them feeling lost and helpless. I have had several family members and friends who have felt as if their whole lives were too difficult as if they could never escape their dire circumstances. In the same fashion, in my own life I have often struggled with my own emotions trying to make sense of something that really was not anything I needed to overthink about so much in the first place.

When I reflect on what so many people whose paths I have crossed have endured as well as my own struggles, I am reminded of how sometimes we encounter angels in disguise which I often refer to as spirit guides. None of us ever really know if someone we encounter could be a special spirit meant to give us hope in the most trying times of our lives. I have truly learned to appreciate unique souls whose paths have crossed mine as often they have said or done something to give me some happiness during a stressful time in my own life.

The following poem, "The Cage and a Kind Spirit Guide", is all about one soul's frustration for feeling trapped in a life that he or she can no longer tolerate. It gives us all a look into one troubled life who gets a chance meeting with a guardian angel of sorts meant to heal him or her of the pain that has been prevalent for way too long. No matter what cage we may feel surrounding us, we should always remember there really are special souls among us all ready and willing to help us feel a renewed sense of joy once again in our lives.

The Cage and a Kind Spirit Guide

I was feeling trapped under a cloak
Of despair not knowing what to do
Then I desperately caught a glimpse of
A spirit guide who cried I am here for you

Reluctant to trust him because
I had been hurt so much
He reached down through the bars of my life
And said the world is cruel but my heart is warm to touch

I was screaming on the inside

Wishing I could just put an end to it all
The spirit guide whispered but you have
To be strong even when you fall

Desperately hoping for a chance to break away
From a life I could no longer stand
The spirit guide smiled with joy and said
You can trust me to never let go of your weary hand

I felt I was spinning in circles wondering when
I could ever leave the life that keep me in chains
The spirit guide whispered there is only so much
Your heart can take when you feel totally ashamed

I was crying on the inside as if
The tears would never seem to end
The spirit guide reached through my cage with
A comforting presence of a much needed friend

I felt I was bouncing off the walls within
A cage that had become my chaotic existence
The spirit guide sensed I needed help and reassurance
With a peace that overcame all my resistance

I felt my eyes were playing tricks on me
Because I had trouble seeing a clear path
Despite all the harsh words that had been spoken
The spirit guide said stay strong and don't look back

Without a care in the world I thought

Maybe my life is too worthless for anyone to need
The spirit guide said even when others reject your kindness
Know God rewards all your good deeds

Afraid to take a step forward I was not sure
If I could ever escape my cage
The spirit guide whispered come walk with me
And I will protect you for the rest of your days

In the midst of my darkness a bright light shined
Into my cage as the door of freedom opened
I walked right into the light with my new friend
Whose acts of kindness were the best words ever spoken

Chapter 13 - The Caged Butterfly on the Path to Freedom

Throughout my life I have always been fascinated with butterflies. Every time I see one flying around me I am in awe of the beauty and freedom they possess. What has always intrigued me even more is just how a butterfly emerges from a dark cocoon as I have often wondered how a caterpillar longs for the moment it can escape the darkness of its protective shell to explore the beautiful aspects of nature at its finest.

The following poem, "The Caged Butterfly Who Found the Path to Freedom", is a story of one butterfly who has unfortunately been trapped in its very own dark cocoon for way too long. When it finally is given the chance to break free, it finds that nobody or nothing can stop it from exploring new horizons. After many long, dark nights of the soul, the butterfly in this narrative poem finally discovers not only a new found freedom but another like-minded butterfly who turns out to be the best friend it could ever have.

This poem is a reminder to all of us that after tough times we will get our wings to fly. Even more importantly, there is always a special friend out there for all of us who does understand what we are dealing with and wants to be there through all the good and bad moments of this life.

The Caged Butterfly Who Found the Path to Freedom

Once upon a time I was a butterfly trapped
In a world that did not make sense
I was praying somehow God would free me
From the cocoon keeping me frustrated and tense

Anytime I tried to move I felt my cocoon
Kept getting smaller and smaller
No matter how hard I tried to escape
My inner distress kept growing taller and taller

In the midst of my darkness I knew I had
To find strength in the midst of my pain
I was trapped in a cocoon of lost hopes
Feeling so broken as if my wings were tainted with shame

In a moment I could stay right where I was
And feel as if the whole world was passing me by

Yet somewhere in my little heart I knew
I had to keep the faith and quit always asking God why

After many long days and nights sleeping with
My eyes wide open hoping I could break free
One day I noticed a little light shining into my
Imprisoned life giving strength to my misery

Through the cold winter of lost hopes
And broken promises and dreams
There was a new light breaking through my cocoon
Helping me know the world is never as it seems

I slowly spread my wings outside the cocoon
That had not always made me feel ok
Within my little weary soul I just knew
A new chapter had begun to help me embrace a better day

As I took flight onto a path that was
Lined with beautiful, colorful flowers
It was if they spoke words of peace to my
Once troubled soul with the most magical of powers

I flew a little further and noticed another
Little yellow butterfly that saw me flying alone
I felt it could sense I needed a trusted friend
To love me forever and help me find a new home

As I flew in countless circles not sure of
Where to take my next turn in life

My new friend kept flying right beside me
Giving me courage to endure any unwelcome strife

We fluttered our wings to nature's calm melodies
On a spring day when the world was at peace
No matter what happened in either of our worlds
We were finally together without any unease

I could fly right to the most loving flower
To nourish my much hungry soul
Then my new friend flew right by my side
Letting me know he loved me too much to ever let me go

Every time I fly high or low on this new path
God gave me the strength to find
I don't lose hope because of the gift of a friend
To keep me strong and from losing my little mind

It is funny how at times in my life
I never thought I would ever survive
Yet with my kindred spirit flying right beside me
I could make it through the worst of times

There are days I am tempted to look back
And reflect on the moments where I felt so trapped
Yet even when I feel lost the love of my new friend
Keeps me from always looking back

I may be just a little butterfly with a once broken spirit
Looking for a place where I could escape

Now I know the treasures that God gives
When He gave me a special friend to help me find a better
way

Chapter 14 - The Day Hope Took the Last Guilt Trip

When I think about guilt trips, I honestly think about how many of these trips I have taken throughout my own life. In fact, I have always allowed myself to get taken in by the deceptive woes of another soul who really just played on my good nature to get me to cater or his or her needs. There have been countless times I have let others manipulate me into doing something I really did not want to do just to make him or her happy. Now that I have gotten older, I have learned to take a lot less of these guilt trips as I always remind myself that I am not responsible for someone else's happiness.

The following poem, "The Day Hope Took the Last Guilt Trip", is a story of a woman named Hope who really always wanted the best for others and herself, yet she went through years of trying to please others only to find herself unhappy in the process.

Just remember that, like Hope, there will be times we face others trying to use a guilt trip of sorts to push us into thinking or doing things a certain way for their benefit. When that happens, we should always remember that we need to value our own thoughts and feelings and not get influenced to do or feel something that goes against what we truly desire and need for our own path in life.

The Day Hope Took the Last Guilt Trip

Hope was always trying to see
The very best of things
Yet there was always a guilt trip
Trying to create too many mysteries

Hope felt she had to quit letting
Everyone bring her down
She decided maybe her luck would get better
And she could escape into a more peaceful town

Hope had been working way too hard
And always did everything to please others so
Somehow she just wanted to take a break
From all the stress and learn how to let go

Hope tried hard to make ends meet
And do exactly what was needed

But in her humble heart she was tired of trying
So hard and feeling completely defeated

Hope had a heart of great warmth even
When the world was cold and dreary
Yet she knew she had to keep the faith
No matter how much she felt weak and weary

Hope knew she had to remain strong
And keep fighting to the end
Even with the rest of the world against
Her soul she believed in the power of a good friend

Hope spent day and night searching
For answers to all of her whys
She knew she could not give up even when
She would rather drown under the world's constant cries

Hope was a good soul who really believed
Her fate would change for the good
Even when the guilt of negative souls surrounded her
She had faith life would work out like it should

Hope was determined to find a happier way of life
Despite unhealthy roads holding her back
Inside of her struggling spirit she was determined
To stay on a more spiritual track

Hope wanted to make sure all her choices
Based on guilt were finally over and gone

Despite the draining energies of unworthy souls
She could overcome the most insensitive wrongs

Hope decided to venture upon the very last guilt trip
She felt like she was destined to take
When this ride was over she embraced a new path
Where she grew stronger from all her past mistakes

Chapter 15 - The Desperate But Healing Heart

Desperation is something that I have often discovered is a sensitive topic to discuss. So many of us find ourselves desperate to feel and do so many things, yet we often feel held back or stripped of the dreams we so long to make come true. I have met many people along the way whose lives have been torn apart so often by feelings of desperation. There is something unsettling about wanting something so much and never really reaching the goals or dreams we have set for ourselves.

Not only have we all known some form of desperation in life, but we all have known heartbreak as so often these two forces of nature go hand in hand. Desperation leads to heartbreak and heartbreak often leads to desperation. Once we have gone through either one, I have discovered how important it truly becomes to embrace spiritual healing so we can learn from the lessons life has taught us.

The following poem, "The Desperate But Healing Heart", discusses the journey of a soul whose struggles in life have created so much sadness and despair, yet this person discovers that there is always hope for better days ahead. Even when our hearts get broken, there is always healing to occur as long as we realize that sometimes we need to ask for help and ask God to give us strength to face another day. In fact, sometimes just knowing there is someone out there to really care for us when we need it most provides the most beautiful healing of all.

The Desperate But Healing Heart

I was searching high and low for
Some way to escape my broken life
Somehow everywhere I turned I was faced
With false promises and unending strife

There were days I looked for answers that
I thought would be easy to find
Yet all I discovered were misguided promises
Causing me to lose my troubled mind

I decided to take a drive down a road
Away from all my stress

No matter where I turned I ran into one roadblock
After the other putting my heart to the test

Frustrated and confused I came to a fork
In the road not sure of where to turn
All I knew was I prayed God would tell me
Which way to go so I would not get burned

In a moment of complete panic I shouted
Out to God to give me a sign
He just whispered from Heaven keep the faith
And your heart will find the answers in time

Still unhappy because every choice I made
In my past seemed to break my heart piece by piece
I asked God to help me choose the right road so
My heart would not feel so weary and weak

Hoping for the answers to come as I stood
At a crossroads that seemed to hold me back
God whispered look deep in your heart
And remember what broke it from the past

I looked within and found myself crying so much
Because of all the hurt I had been through
Somehow I could not figure out why when
I thought I found love it proved to be far from true

I looked a little deeper in my heart hoping
I could find the key to make the right choices

But somewhere in the midst of my weary spirit
All I could hear were chaotic voices

There were echoes of words from so many
Claiming they would always be there
Yet when I looked deeper these same souls
Ran away showing me they only pretended to care

With tears in my eyes and my hand
Over my troubled heart
I begged God to give me
A much needed fresh, new start

He said look a little deeper and remember
I sent a rainbow after all your storms
When others hurt you deeply I sent a warm feeling
Of hope to keep your heart from further harm

I realized standing at this crossroads that
All the pain I endured happened for a reason
Somehow God wanted me to see my heart
Had grown stronger through every passing season

I still was not sure what road I needed to take
To heal my heart and move on with my dreams
God just said when you follow your heart
You will find the right love waiting for you so patiently

I thought I could take the road of security
Just to please others who knew me well

But God said don't go there for I had lived too long
Without real love and with no magical stories to tell

As I took a deep breath I felt my heart beat stronger
As I leaned in the direction it wanted me to go
When I turned down the road of new beginnings
I felt closer to the love God meant for me to know

When I made the choice to follow
My desperate but healing heart
I knew that God helped me make the right choice
To embrace a love that would not let me fall apart

The journey I was now traveling was one where
My heart felt it was finding a place to call home
As I kept looking forward my heart felt stronger now
As it got closer to the arms of its kindred soul

Chapter 16 - The Echo of a Broken Soul Searching for Direction

If there is one thing that I have come to learn in my life, it is to never assume that someone is okay when really he or she may not be. Sometimes we all assume that if someone is feeling good on the outside that he or she must be feeling the same on the inside. Even though that may be true at times for some of us, I know the opposite is often the case. We should never assume that someone is always doing great because sometimes the ones we think are happiest often are hiding the greatest pain.

I know depression is something so many of us experience at one point or another in life, but many times our very own family members and friends and even ourselves fall victim to depression's suffocating hold over our hearts and minds. It has always upset me when people underestimate depression as I know from personal experience in my own life how hard it can be, but as I have learned there is always hope and a better way. We must not lost heart and trust God that everything will work out the best for us.

The following poem, "The Echo of A Broken Soul Searching for Direction", is all about a soul who is battling the dark forces of depression and is truly in need of hope that things will get better.

The Echo of A Broken Soul Searching for Direction

I was running like mad trying
To keep track of it all
Before I knew what hit me
I took a sudden fall

I asked God to help me
Try to stay on track
Then those energy vampires
Come again pulling me under attack

I feel at times like I am drowning in
A sea of confusion I can't control
I wonder if the darkness of life is
Suffocating my heart too tight to let it go

There are times I just feel like
I have so much to do

Just when I get a handle on things
My calm composure begins to come unglued

Sometimes I take a walk and wonder
What it would take for me to die
I feel the happy face I portray is just covering
Up the truth of my soul that just wants to cry

There are times I look up into the sky
Wondering if I could just fly away
I wonder if anyone would really miss me
Or just the way they use me to get their way

At times I just do not think I have the strength
To keep fighting because life seems so tough
I find myself once again caught in the grip
Of another case of bad luck

My life has always been an up and down
Battle with depression
Even when things are good my soul soon finds itself
Struggling to learn a much needed lesson

I feel as if my spirit is at war with the
Very essence of who God created me to be.
On the outside I appear strong and confident
But on the inside I feel relentless misery

I'm not sure if I will ever catch my breath
Long enough to crawl out of the pit of despair

I just would like for once someone to do something
Really nice for me to show me they care

In the dark of night, I escape into a dream where
I feel everything is working out for the best
It is like God's way of rewarding me with
A new life where I feel I can finally find serene rest

Some days I feel I have a passion that
Can conquer the entire world with just a smile
Then something chokes my inner voice and
Keeps me feeling I am not that worthwhile

The echo of a broken soul is like a song
Without the right music to bring it to life
When I listen to my inner voice
I find God wanting to help me find a way past my strife

No matter where I go and no matter
How hard I try to hide
God knows I need healing to take place
To find the strength to find joy on the inside

Chapter 17 - The Flower Garden of Tranquility

Peace is something that I feel we all long to embrace and experience in this life. Sometimes it can be very hard to find true peace with all the chaos and distractions that surround us. There are times we just need to take a time out for ourselves and really get away from the the external and internal noise that often causes us distress. Sometimes just taking a break from it all does the heart and soul very good because we need a chance to refresh and renew our energy so we can keep going.

The following poem, "The Flower Garden of Tranquility", is all about how one soul gets to escape the stresses of life in a dream finding himself or herself walking among many rows of various colorful flowers. In fact, this dream is a reflection of Heaven, and it is as if God has given the person in the poem a chance to experience enough tranquility so that he or she can wake up with a brand new determination to face his or her obstacles knowing there will be enough spiritual protection to overcome them.

Remember peace is something we should always embrace because no matter where or how you experience it, finding a tranquil way to release stress is something all of our hearts and souls desire.

The Flower Garden of Tranquility

I fell deep in a dream down a staircase
Leading to a most magical place
I never realized I was meant to get away
From it all and go inward so I could finally escape

After days and nights of much turmoil
I woke up in a garden full of colorful flowers
Somehow I could feel that God was going
To speak to my soul with great spiritual powers

There were rows of red roses
So eager to get my attention
They whispered it was time I allowed destiny
To help me make the right decision

I looked around and saw a line of daisies
Dancing together in the most harmonic embrace

I could feel them sending me energy that
My tough times would lead to even happier days

I got back on my feet to be greeted by some
Pink tulips that smelled so sweet and true
I heard them gently echo the words it is
Time to let life be good to you

I walked in another direction in this garden
Where I stumbled across some lucky carnations
With one sweet smell I felt they gave me
Better luck to overcome my present tribulations

As I was starting to feel better
Some yellow daffodils caught my eye
They brought a smile to my face as they knew
How to give my weary soul more strength to try

Feeling as if maybe my fate would change
And my life would not be so stressful
I then ran across a section of lilies whose
Lovely aura made me feel more restful

Curious to see what else this
Special garden had in store for me
My eyes caught a glimpse of sunflowers
With a message of hope to help me overcome my misery

As I looked around the garden of tranquility
I knew I really did not want to walk away

Yet somehow I felt these flowers where a sign from God
That I was destined to find a better way

I got down on my knees asking God to help me
Face the world again without fear of a new direction
As my dream ended flower petals from the garden
Surrounded my heart with spiritual protection

Chapter 18 - The Forgiving Tree

Forgiveness is one of the most challenging concepts to embrace. We have all been hurt, and we have all wanted to make sure whomever hurt us pays the price for what he or she did. It's human nature to want to get back at the person who did us wrong. After all, nothing is more unsettling than seeing the person who caused hurt get away with his or her dirty deeds.

Over the course of my lifetime, I have witnessed family members and friends hold on to such bitterness towards another person for some injustice. Rather than taking the high road to forgive that person, I have observed how holding a grudge can truly build a wall between the person needing forgiveness and the one who should offer to forgive. Even though I have endured many hurtful experiences throughout my life, I have always tried to forgive the person who hurt me. It may not have been easy, but it is so much better to let go of pain rather than hold on to it. Holding on to hurt only creates more pain, but choosing to forgive truly frees the heart and soul from further misery.

The following poem, "The Forgiving Tree", is a narrative poem that tells the story of someone who befriends an isolated tree whose branches have been worn down by many years of hard times. In this story the tree is rather bitter at all the creatures and forces of nature that have cause it so much pain. Luckily, the person who finds the tree helps it realize that the only way it can keep growing stronger and survive is to forgive all of the things that kept it feeling broken in the first place. This poem illustrates that true forgiveness brings healing to the heart and soul.

The Forgiving Tree

I was walking in a field with waves
Of grain swaying from side to side
When all of a sudden a lonely tree stripped
Of its leaves caught my eye

I walked a little closer to get a better look
At this tree that seemed all alone
I said you seem a little sad and in need of
A good friend that you can call your own

This little tree cried out how I do I know
I can trust what you say

Everyone I ever cared about stripped me
Of a leaf and a limb or two along the way

I decided to sit down in front of this tree
Because I felt it had so much to share
Then I whispered I really value the heart
Of you when so many others did not care

I asked this little tree what had happened
To make it hurt so much
It just screamed look at my weary limbs and
They will show you wounds I can't seem to give up

The little tree went on to say take a look at
One of my limbs that has no bark to keep it safe
When I asked why, he said because I let others
Tell me I was not good enough and just a disgrace

With tears in my eyes I said what else
Has happened to make you so brittle
The tree shouted out my trunk has been hurt by others
Casting stones at me for they are so bitter

I could not believe someone could be so cruel
So I asked my new friend to tell me more
He whispered you cannot swing from my branches
Because they are too weak from life's storms

I was full of sadness and asked the little tree
If its leaves had changed colors in the fall

He just cried my leaves never got to shine brightly
Because a thief in the night stole them all

In such despair I asked the little tree
How it was able to stand so strong
He just exclaimed I have had nobody to be there
To help me make right all of nature's wrongs

In that moment I knew that God was the great healer
Speaking through me to help my friend
I held my arms out widely and embraced his little trunk
That seem cold and in need of life again

He said why are you hugging me when everyone
And everything else has hurt me so much
I said because I want you to feel the healing power
Of God's love that is true with His divine touch

All of a sudden there came a soft rain that was
Actually tears falling from the tree's top branches
The little tree was sobbing why is it when I provided
Shade to others they took advantage of all my circumstances

I just kept hugging the tree and said I want you
To feel the very beat of my own loving heart
The tree just said you seem so strong and here
You are helping me embrace a brand new start

With such confusion, this lonely tree could not
Understand why I cared so much for his soul

Even through words unspoken I could feel
His troubled energy crying out please don't let me go

The more the tears of this special tree came
Pouring down on me as I embraced him tighter
I just prayed out to God to help my friend forgive
Those who hurt him so his heart would feel so much lighter

As the rain came to an end and the sun pierced
Through the clouds on that cool, fall day
I noticed there were all kinds of colored leaves around
The tree's trunk that were special in so many ways

In that moment I could feel the little tree
Smiling at me as its branches swayed to and fro
When the magical colored leaves appeared I know he had
Forgiven his hurts and found a true friend in me that would
never let him go

Chapter 19 - The Game of Addiction

The power of addiction is a battle that so many of us face. It can so hard to overcome addictions to certain things that seem to want to keep us a prisoner to our own pain. No matter what we do sometimes or where we turn, trying to overcome an addiction is often one of the greatest struggles we will ever face.

I have had my own struggles with certain addictions throughout my life, and I can honestly say the only way I was able to overcome them was through lots of prayer and spiritual strength. First of all, we have to be willing to own the fact we have an addiction. Then only God is the one along with supportive family and friends to give us the ability to help break an addictive hold over our lives.

The following poem, "The Game of Addiction", gives true

insight into the psychological effects an addiction can have upon someone else's life. Even though at times it may seem hopeless to try and overcome it, the key is believing in oneself and trusting in God to give us the courage we need to rise above addiction's suffocating hold.

The Game of Addiction

I was walking along a path that
Seemed too hard for me to endure
Yet I could not resist the enticing charms held
For me leaving me completely lost and unsure

I thought maybe I could just walk around
The things keeping me so addicted
Yet somehow I could not escape a life
Where I felt totally restricted

There were moments in my past
I wish I could get back
Then before I knew what to do
I was falling right off track

Some addictive moments I thought
Were some of my best times
Yet on the outside I played it safe while
The rest of the time I was dying inside

I thought it would be good to
Take my chances with fate

Yet I found myself losing sight
Of myself with every mistake

There were scary memories flooding
My soul that almost tore me apart
But no matter what I did I could not shake
The feeling of how those addictions broke my heart

Despite the need I have inside to give up
A life that keeps bringing me down
The lure of addictive gemstones has a knack
For turning my smiles right into a frown

I thought there has to come a time when
I can breathe without feeling such pressure
Yet it seems just when I get some fresh air
I feel lost again like an abandoned treasure

The mystic pull of addictions in my life
Have always kept me feeling weak
I can be doing so well and then another addiction
Hits me leaving me drowning in a world of defeat

I just keep hoping maybe there is another way
To end the addictive games that play with my mind
Somehow though I find myself too weary to
Overcome the nature of these crazy times

With every step I take down
The path that I feel is right for me

Another addiction from the past or present
Remains determined to isolate me in misery

I feel like I am trapped in a prison
Of my own misguided making
I'm foolish for giving into the addictive pleasures
Of a life from which I need to feel awakened

Looking back and moving forward
Is not always so easy to do
If I could give up the addictive nature of myself
I could live a life so authentic and true

In the midst of my frustration I know
I have to keep the faith all will be ok
I have learned to trust that with every addictive
Mistake God will help me find a better way

Chapter 20 - The Heart That Cried for Help

The human heart is something that I have always admired and yet misunderstood so many times. I have seen so many people living their lives as if nothing or nobody could ever bring them down. It was as if they felt they were invincible in a such a way where nothing could hurt them. However, eventually what happens are those good times can change on a dime bringing lots of frustration and pain. It is during these times, that the human heart is always put to the most challenging of tests forcing us all to question our purpose in life.

Because the human heart struggles so often, I think so many of us feel as if we are only halfway living. At times it seems on the outside our lives our wonderful, yet on the inside a very different story could be taking place. The human heart is capable of so much great love and joy, and yet when in distress, it can affect our human spirit in the most challenging of ways as we question why so many bad things often happen to the best people.

The following poem, "The Heart That Cried for Help", is all about one human heart who is living his or her life to please others making everyone think he or she has it all together. However, the reality of this human heart is that it is in great pain and is feeling desperate to break away from all his or her struggles just to find some true peace and happiness.

The Heart That Cried for Help

My heart was screaming on the inside
When would it ever end
I was tired of broken dreams and false promises
That kept haunting me over and over again

Every day was a struggle to break free
Of a life I no longer wanted
Yet no matter which way I turned I was chained to a world
Whose negativity kept my spirit haunted

I was so tired of pretending to be everything
Everyone always wanted me to be
All I needed was a break from frustrating
Circumstances so I could find the real me

It seemed that everyday I tried to write a new
Beginning something would keep be down
What I really needed was inspiration beyond measure
So I could find the strength to stay around

My stomach was churning in knots as if I could
Never find the peace I needed to survive
Somehow I could barely take another step before
My heart broke again causing me to cry

I have spent so many years trying to reach
My goals but never reaching them all
Maybe I could just run away to a far away island
Before my heart takes the final fall

Everyone thinks I am such a free spirit yet
They really don't see my heart is in great pain
I have been lost in a world where truth
No longer exists and my spirit is drowning in shame

There are so many times I have wished
That I could just run away
Sometimes I am not sure my heart can take
Another disappointment ruining another hopeful day

I have prayed countless prayers asking God
To give me strength not to give up
Yet my very human heart can only take so much
Before it cries out it has had enough

Tears stream down my face so often because
I feel trapped in places I cannot escape
Yet I feel the touch of a spiritual angel
Holding my heart so I do not fall from grace

This heart of mine that still cries for help
Is often abused and pulled in confusing directions
But I have learned to keep the faith that
Through my struggles I will learn great lessons

Chapter 21 - The Heartbreak That Never Seems to End

Let's face it. At some point in all of our lives we are going to be faced with some type of heartbreak. It would be so nice if we could just go through life without ever having conflicts with the people in our lives. However, conflict is an inevitable part of this life. As hard as it is, sometimes it teaches us great lessons.

What is even more challenging than conflict, is learning to cope with the betrayal of someone who we thought cared and who we felt could be trusted. We have all faced various types of betrayal, and sometimes even when we try to make amends the other party involved may not want to make things right with us. When that happens, I have learned it is best to forgive and yet walk away when you know you have done all you can to restore a broken relationship.

The following poem, "The Heartbreak That Never Seems to End", is a poem about two people who were once very good friends, yet due to conflict and misunderstandings they were never able to reconcile their friendship. Eventually, after one friend's failed attempts to restore the friendship despite some signs of improvement, he or she realizes that it was more heartbreaking trying to reestablish a friendship again with false hopes and promises when clearly the other person was really no longer receptive. Heartbreak over a broken relationship of any kind is never easy, but the lesson here is that it's ok to let go knowing we did our part to make things right.

The Heartbreak that Never Seems to End

I was strolling right along feeling
Like everything was finally going ok
Then I ran right into you
Not knowing what to say

You looked at me with eyes
That seemed to say I really do care
You even made me feel all was forgiven
And you wanted to really clear the air

For just a brief moment you made me think
You wanted to be my friend

It was if you had forgiven the past between us
And wanted to really make amends

I even shared how sorry
I was for my past mistakes
Yet you acted like you understood but kept
Me at arm's length with your distant ways

It is funny how I remember standing in front of you
Once again looking like a complete fool
You made me think we could be friends again and yet
You cut me off again leaving me so confused

I do not think I will ever understand why you acted
As if the friendship was something you missed
Yet you made it clear that your boundaries would remain
And it was obvious with you our friendship had been
dismissed

There are times that I wonder why I even tried
To give you the time of day at all
Once again I remain the wounded victim of your lies
And was set up to take the fall

I have prayed over and over again for God to give me
The strength to forgive you for how you hurt me
Yet somehow no matter how much I think you have healed
You seem to throw another dagger into my heart so
relentlessly

I walked away from you thinking to myself
Why did I even allow you back into my world
You just hurt me all over again with what I thought
Were true actions contradicted by your false words

There is only so much pain any one of us can take
When someone wounds our soul
I know that for as long as I live I will be careful
And hope that God will finally help me let you go

Chapter 22 - The Magician With The Deceptive Heart

Every now and then we think we have found a true friend who will be there and support us no matter what happens. Sometimes we discover that the friend we thought was true is often a false friend in disguise using various forms of manipulation to try and get us to say or do something that is for that person's benefit rather than our own.

I have often found myself in this situation where I trusted the wrong person who I thought had my best interests at heart but who in all truth just wanted to use me for his or her personal gain. To this day, I am very cautious about who I trust and call a friend because not everyone is worthy of that title.

The following poem, "The Magician With The Deceptive

Heart", is all about the charm and yet destructive nature of having a false friend. So many people can make us think they are true blue and that we can trust in them no matter what. However, we could all benefit from learning to trust our instincts. If someone or something seems too good to be true, then chances are that is the reality of the situation. It is always good to be friendly, but we all need to be extra careful regarding who we allow to be our friends.

The Magician With The Deceptive Heart

My spirit was getting stronger
And stronger day by day
Then you came back into my life
With your lies and misguided ways

I should have known better than
To trust your words were true
All I ever did was be
A faithful friend to you

In one moment you were
As nice as you could be
I could look right into your eyes and
Know you were trying to be a friend to me

In the next minute I said
I was sorry for things I had done
Yet instead of admitting your own faults you blamed
Me again for being out of line and out of touch

There was a brief moment in time
When I thought your sincerity seemed real
Yet as soon as I fell into your trap of deceit
My heart realized you cared less about my good will

I thought we had come
To some meeting of the minds
But as soon as I extended my forgiveness you
Rejected my friendship with words that were so unkind

I looked you right in the eye trying to figure out
Why you made me think you were so right
It was obvious I was all at fault and
You remained so prideful and uptight

When I walked away I could not believe
I ever thought you changed
The more I thought about your careless words
I realized I needed to finally walk away

In the quiet of the night I cried so much
I felt my heart was going to completely break
I found myself once again the misguided fool
Falling for your fake friendly ways

It has been many months since
I let you first wound my weary soul
Just when I find my strength again you hurt me
So much I hope this time I can finally let you go

It is funny how strange life can be when we think
Someone we once trusted really does care
Yet the reality is that sometimes wolves in sheep's clothing
Stay trapped in a world smothered by cold air

I am so angry with myself for letting you
Trick me into thinking you were truly a friend
With help from God, I pray I can find the strength
To open up my heart and trust again

Chapter 23 - The Pieces of the Puzzle Called Life

Ever since I was a little girl, I have always been fascinated by the concept of puzzles. I can remember staring at the puzzle box picture wondering how to make all the pieces fit together so I could create the picture perfect image that was staring right back at me. I then would do all I could to find the right pieces of the puzzle so I could somehow make the picture I saw just like the box portrayed.

At this point when I reflect back on those puzzles that seemed so perfect, I often find myself trying to piece together pieces of a puzzle in my own life that often don't make sense. Sometimes I think it may be easy to find a way to piece life together again when everything seems like it is falling apart. However, I have learned that not all the pieces go back together again so easily. Sometimes pieces get lost and the picture perfect scene we imagine does not always come together quite the way we hope it to be.

The following poem, "The Pieces of the Puzzle Called Life", reflect the nature of trying to put the pieces of broken dreams and promises back together again when it seems all hope is lost.

The Pieces of the Puzzle Called Life

All through my life I had worked
Puzzles great and small
Yet somehow the pieces never seemed to fit
And I could not complete the puzzle of life at all

There was one puzzle God gave me
Where it seemed all the pieces never seemed to fit
But no matter how I looked at it I knew there was
A lesson to learn telling me not to quit

I found another puzzle where the pieces
Were hard to place together
Yet the more I looked at the big picture
I could tell my soul was destined to live forever

I started looking around to find the pieces
Of the puzzle for my restless mind
But I just found rugged edges that almost fit
But were not in sync to my puzzle's needed rhyme

In my deepest moments of distress I discovered
A puzzle where there was a rainbow after the rain
When I put all the pieces together I could tell God
Was leading me on a new path far from pain

During trying times I tried to work a puzzle
Where all the pieces painted a picture of great art
Even when there was a piece or two missing I knew
It was a sign to heal my wounded heart

I could walk outside and work a puzzle to
Understand nature's greatest mysteries
In the depths of my spirit I could feel the pieces
I used were in harmony with my soul's chemistry

There were stormy days when I tried to work
A puzzle that was totally hard to understand
Yet I still held onto the sharp pieces trying to
Wound me with the strength of my own weary hands

In times when I felt I needed a complete break
From stress and frustrating commotion
I knew the pieces from my past were the learning links
To face the present puzzle with much devotion

I could walk through every store in town
Admiring the puzzles calling me by name
Somehow they held the mystic lessons I was meant
To learn to keep my unsettled energies more tame

I decided one day that maybe it was time to look
Within to solve the hardest puzzle I ever faced.
This one required much soul searching and
The need to follow my heart along the way

When I look at all the times when
The answers were not there
I reached for the piece of the puzzle where God
Whispered you know I will always care

Then I could feel that my heart was not
Quite where it wanted to be
But I reached for the piece of the puzzle that calmed
My fears like a sweet, loving musical melody

When I looked at all the times my soul
Was tired and so weary
I found a piece of the puzzle that seemed to
Enlighten my own life like a beautiful love story

The more I searched deep within, the more I knew
The pieces of my life's puzzle would be complete
I kept the faith knowing all the pieces would
Come together and lead me on a path of forever peace

Chapter 24 - The Raging River of Fear

Fear is probably one of the most real and yet difficult of emotions. The more we hold onto fear, the harder it can be to face all of the challenges that lie before us.

I have endured many fears throughout my lifetime wondering if certain things I had hoped for were going to work out. I feared so much for so long that I found myself wondering if I would ever be able to make it sometimes from point A to point B.

Over the course of time, I have come to learn that fear is not always a bad thing as long as we don't cave under the pressure of thinking there is no way out and that we are destined to stay in a bad situation. One thing I have come to understand is that life is all about facing our fears and knowing that no matter how dangerous fear can be that God always has our back.

The following poem, "The Raging River of Fear", is all about realizing that we are strong enough to conquer our fears as long as we don't lose hope.

The Raging River of Fear

I was floating down the raging river of fear
Not sure of what I should do
It seemed everywhere I looked there were
Obstacles trying to scare me through and through

In so many ways I thought maybe I could hold onto
A tree that seemed rooted in great strength
Yet somehow the unpredictable river of fear
Kept me on an unbalanced kind of wavelength

There were storms hitting left and right
Trying to blow me down
No matter where I turned I could feel my inner fears
Were trying to create chaos all around

I wanted to just hide out under a rock
Where nobody could ever find me
Maybe I could escape into a world of refuge
Where I could escape such misery

Throughout so many times in my life I thought
This raging river would cease to exist

I just wish I could find a peaceful place to
Escape that was much easier than this

It is hard to pretend to the world
That everything is always ok
I would like to float down this river where
All my blues could just float away

In times of great despair and times when
The world seems somewhat at peace
Something always seems to happen to disturb
My balanced state with an upsetting kind of tease

Not always sure of what I can do and not knowing
When the treacherous river of fear will stop
There are only so many times I can hit the rocks
Of frustration before my weary heart stops

If I could make one wish that would put my life
Back on the path of much greater hope
Maybe when the harsh waters of the river
Of fear attack me I will eventually be able to cope

Somehow I am not sure how long I can journey
Down this river without drowning under such pain
There are times I need to find a place to call home
That does not put my struggling mind to shame

I wonder when the raging river of fear will become
One where peace finally reigns supreme

Being true to myself is the hardest battle I have fought
But it keeps me strong and free from shame

During the cloudy days when it is hard to
Really see a way that is truly clear
I know that I cannot completely escape a world
That is completely free from my constant fears

As the raging river of fear continues
To keep me swaying to and fro
Somehow I know that God will be the anchor
To keep me strong without ever letting me go

Chapter 25 - The Shadows of an Exhausted Spirit

Exhaustion is truly something that I feel we all know very well. It is one thing to be physically tired after a long day at work or even when we are unable to get a good night's rest. However, it's another thing to feel completely emotionally drained after we have given so much of ourselves time and time again.

I often battle a very weary spirit that seems to stay tired so often. I used to think that maybe I had something truly wrong since it seemed I could get a full night of sleep and still wake up like I never had slept at all. What I came to realize and understand is that exhaustion of the spirit can really make us or break us. We can choose to let the stresses of this life overtake us or we can fight to keep going and to keep working hard no matter what odds we come up against.

The following poem, "The Shadows of an Exhausted Spirit", talk of one weary soul's journey to stay strong in life despite all the forces of nature that he or she was not expecting to face. It's a poem about surviving no matter how hard this life may get.

The Shadows of an Exhausted Spirit

I struggle so very often to try to
Stay on top of this crazy world
Yet each time I start to feel great
Shadows in my life leave me feeling lost and hurt

I often try to ignore the fact that
I have been a victim of depression
But the shadows of my past often rear their ugly head
To teach me an unwanted lesson

Sometimes I feel so tired that
I just want to give up
But even when I am too weak to
Face a day I ask God to help me hang tough

There are times I know that the smile
On the outside of me is not how I truly feel
I am just afraid if I don't hold on to it I may
Lose touch with the part of me that wants to be real

When I look within my heart I feel that
Maybe my past has left me broken and weary
Yet within my frustrated spirit I have to keep
Fighting to keep from feeling so dreary

Many times I wonder if the shadows
Of the past will ever leave me alone
I am so sick of letting negative energy get the
Better of me when my heart wants a positive home

I often want to cry my eyes out because
I just wish my luck would change
The shadows of constant misfortune in my past
Keep trying to haunt my good name

I have lived so much of my life trying
To be what everyone else thought I should be
But all those years of trying to please others
Left me feeling alone in a sea of misery

No matter how hard I try to make
My life the absolute best
I just keep wishing the shadows of false promises
Would let me get some much needed rest

There are days I look within to try and
Move past everything that has gone wrong
I know one day fate will change in my favor
And good karma will play me an even happier song

The shadows of past struggles try
To keep me feeling sad and blue
But somewhere I have learned to hope that
With the bad there comes great times too

All my life I have been chasing so many shadows
That want to keep my free spirit down
When the negative energy of hopeless dreams
Tries to attack me I wish I could just leave town

Despite the shadows that seem determined
To keep my spirit drowning in exhaustion
I know I have to stay hopeful that one day
I can let my true self free without acting with such caution

It is amazing to me when I look back over all the
Times I have been so tired I just wanted to cry
Yet in my highest and lowest moments God surrounds me
With a spiritual love I can trust to never die

Chapter 26 - The Teddy Bear in the Toybox of Lost Dreams

Ever since I was a little girl, I have always been fascinated with teddy bears. I loved stuffed animals growing up and often would keep one by my side to help me sleep at night. When I was a kid, I would always hug these teddy bears with such great love as I felt they were full of such joy and goodness.

However, now that I am older I can look at teddy bears being sold in stores or laying around in someone's home just waiting for someone somewhere to give them life again. It's like I can sense that maybe teddy bears are just like the rest of us. They are all searching for someone somewhere to hold them close and comfort them. Just because they seem soft and nice on the outside does not always mean they are truly happy all the time on the inside. In the same fashion, we all can wear the mask that everything is going great when truly our entire world could be falling apart.

In my quest to understand the nature of teddy bears better, I came to realize that sometimes they may feel distressed too and just need to know someone truly cares. The following poem, "The Teddy Bear in the ToyBox of Lost Dreams", reflects the story of a teddy bear just hoping to find solace in the midst of difficult times. Maybe just maybe that teddy bear we have not hugged in a long time could be in a need of a touch of true love and healing.

The Teddy Bear in the Toybox of Lost Dreams

Once upon a time there lived a teddy bear
Full of such life and a desire to stay strong
Yet he wished he could get through one day
Not feeling so pulled apart or like he was made to feel wrong

Some days it was all he could do to
Make it through all the tough times
He would shed a tear and wonder how he could
Escape those who were untrustworthy and unkind

This little teddy bear could feel he was pulled in
Directions where he was not sure he should go
Everyone around him thought they knew him best
Yet he wanted to run away to free his restless soul

One day he found himself lying in the corner
Of a room looking all around
He wondered to himself if I just hide out here
Maybe I can be safe and not feel like I must leave town

In so many ways this teddy bear knew
He wanted to help others when it was his turn
Yet deep in his heart he felt too weak and
Had to heal before he got burned

There were some days he felt like
He needed a really special hug
Then some nights would come when all he wanted
Was to drown out the world with a strong drug

No matter where he turned he never could seem
To find a solution for all of his frustrations
And somewhere in the midst of his unsettled mind
He felt lost in the toybox of desperation

Some days he just would lay awake on the little bed
Where he often could find some release
Yet he really wanted to cry so much because
His heart was breaking and needed so much relief

As one day faded into the next and life seemed
To be one struggle after the other with such stress
The teddy bear just prayed and asked God to protect him
And help him find a place where he could rest

Every night the teddy bear would try to sleep hoping
That in his dreams he could find some peace
No matter how he tossed and turned in the astral world
He could finally be strong and feel free

The teddy bear knew that his life was not meant
To be like all the other teddy bears he knew
He was placed in the toybox of desperation
So his heart and soul would be tried but forever true

There are some teddy bears that seem to have
Everything the world could ever desire
Yet this teddy bear was left feeling all alone and
Wondering if his hopes would ever transpire

The little teddy bear lost in the toybox of desperation
Hoped to find the key to unlock his destiny
With a heart in need of a lucky break he prayed
And asked God to grant him a brand new journey

27

Chapter 27 - Trapped

I have spent alot of my life holding in many of my frustrations as I felt so often that the world felt like it was closing in around me. Sometimes I wondered just how long I could endure a situation when it felt like all hope was lost.

It is so true how sometimes we all just feel we are being suffocated by the demands of this life. We often wonder just how much more we can take until we reach our complete breaking point. I have learned it's ok for all of us to feel the need to break free from the restrictions in life that hold us back and keep us down. No matter what happens, I do not feel God wants any of us to live our lives unhappily.

In the following poem, "Trapped", the focus is upon a lost soul torn apart by despair and stress, yet through all the problems that come this soul realizes everything will be ok as the light is always much stronger than the dark.

Trapped

I felt completely lost in a world
I so no longer wanted
Echoes of false promises and misguided
Charms kept my spirit ever so haunted

My life had become a toy that I felt was
At the mercy of other people's demands
Yet some how some way all I really wanted
Was a real friend who truly understands

I felt bounced around as if I was a ping pong ball
You could hit here and there
There were so many hurtful situations piling up
Around me it made it hard for me to care

No matter which way I turned and no matter
What road I decided to travel
As soon as I start feeling ok again my world
Always seems to come unraveled

In the privacy of my room I could cry myself to sleep
And nobody would ever know I am in pain
Sometimes I wish I could just start all over again
And ask God to keep my restless spirit more tame

So many nights I have worried myself sick

Wondering how long I would feel so upset
Maybe God would send me a angel to let me know
My time of happiness has just not come yet

Everyday I feel I am truly the star of
A drama that really is not me
I just feel trapped by broken dreams and false hopes
That have my spirit drowning in sympathy

Sometimes I wonder if this world would be
A much better place if I kept from feeling so confused
Yet I just keep going all the time like a robot in motion
Hoping to escape from a spirit always feeling so used

Many times I feel that I am on a race track
Headed to a destination that scares me so
I wish with all my heart I could release the lock
On my spirit and let my good energy flow

There is only so much in the story of life
That one person can take
My regrets have often clouded the lessons
I was meant to learn from all my mistakes

I hope one day I can finally escape the life
That has me feeling so trapped
With help from God I hope things will get better
As long as I keep going and don't look back

Chapter 28 - Waking Up Tired

There have been so many times I have fought to wake up feeling as if I could face the world without any problem, and there have been times I thought that I could overcome any hardship or obstacle that came my way. However, there have been many times that despite my inner strength I could barely make it out of bed in the morning.

All my life I have struggled with bouts of depression, and I have learned that it can make me feel so utterly wiped out when I just need some strength to face another day. Depression is a hard thing for any of us to face, yet it is also the reason we find ourselves waking up tired because it so hard to pretend all is well when you just struggle to keep going.

The following poem, "Waking Up Tired", is all about the

struggles we face when depression tries to get the better of our soul, yet it offers hope that greater days are waiting for us just around the corner.

Waking Up Tired

I stumbled out of bed wondering
What in the world I should do
It was like all my past mistakes had me
Searching for something honest and true

I tried and tried to figure out
How it all went wrong
I realized despite trying to fit in
I was meant to sing my own unique song

Everyday had become a struggle
Just for me to get through
I decided maybe I needed to enroll
In a life course 101 kind of school

Each morning I rubbed my eyes hoping
Something good would come my way
I was so tired of dragging through life
While my heart was wasting away

No matter how early I went to bed
I never seemed to get the rest I needed
My soul was weighed down by distress
And a spirit feeling defeated

I thought maybe I could lose myself
In a dream hoping it would not end
Yet as another day began I would still be
Seeking the comfort of a most trusted friend

Everywhere I looked I felt pulled
In so many confusing directions
I just wanted to run away and lose myself
In a world free of heartless rejections

I did not understand why I had to wake
Up feeling I could not keep it together
Most days I could relate to the unpredictable
Winds that contributed to harsh weather

I was waking up every day of my existence
Feeling my life had still not begun
Falling into the safe treasures of my heart
Was a prize my soul still had not won

Sometimes I think about why life falls
Into place for others and not for me
I figured if I rubbed my eyes enough
My present chaos would change into a symphony

Waking up tired is a constant battle
My heart and soul continue to fight
I pray each morning God gives me
The strength to just get through another night

Chapter 29 - Mr. High Hopes and Wolves in Sheep's Clothing

If there is one thing that I have learned in life, it is to always trust my instincts. When it comes to the idea that some people and some things are not always what they seem, I have learned to trust that gut feeling. In fact, one of my favorite sayings to family and friends is to be aware that there are many wolves in sheep's clothing out there.

I have made the mistake in my past way too many times trusting the wrong people. If only I had listened to my instincts warning me to be cautious I might have avoided the problems that resulted. I used to think that everyone had my best interests at heart, but when any of us get hurt, we quickly realize that just being able to find one true blue soul in the midst of all the dark ones out there is definitely a blessing.

The following poem, "Mr. High Hopes and Wolves in Sheep's Clothing", is all about being mindful that not everyone who calls him or herself friend is always deserving of that title. However, when we find a trustworthy, honest soul we should always make sure our paths remain in harmony as knowing someone truly cares is the best gift to receive in a world full of deceptive energies.

Mr. High Hopes and Wolves in Sheep's Clothing

One upon a time Mr. High Hopes was looking
All around for a sheep to call his own
Somehow everywhere he went
He felt lost in a world gone cold

He thought there has to be some sheep
Out there that he can fully trust
Yet somehow all he found are the ones who
Misled his heart and left him in the dust

He used his powers of perception to try and
Understand the clever wolves in his midst
They reeled him in and spit him out as if they
Wanted him to see how much he would risk

Something inside of him was so desperate
To expose so much dark deception
He looked at all the wolves in sheep's clothing
Hoping to give them a dose of healthy rejection

When he was a child he learned
Quickly to always count his sheep
Yet he often found an image of a sheep gone
Bad that kept him from falling asleep

Everyday he took a long look around to
Find some sheep with a good intention
There always seemed to be one out there
Lost like him looking for a new creative vision

When he compared all those good sheep to
The ones his heart just can't fully understand
He knew there are those with the purest of spiritual energy
Whose heart was orchestrated by God's plan

Somehow he was not sure which way was
Always the best route for him to take
He just knew he was tired of trusting the wrong sheep
Just so a wolf could keep him in harm's way

From one maze to the next he was trying
To get away from the persona of evil
He could feel the the deceptive disguises of other sheep
Were keeping him in a state of upheaval

Out of desperation he prayed and asked God
To give him some much needed relief
He just wanted to know there was one sheep
Without a hidden agenda who would not cause him grief

Mr. High Hopes was worried he was trapped in a cage
With the wolves in sheep's clothing forever
But he prayed God would protect his soul with
A peaceful sheep his heart could always treasure

Chapter 30 - The Honest Apple

Of all the virtues in this life, the one that I truly treasure the most is honesty. I don't think anything is more beautiful than someone or something presenting an image in a truthful light. The sad thing is sometimes we all have to encourage alot of dishonest souls and situations before we are made aware of just how good it feels to hear and feel the truth.

Despite all the mistakes I have made along the way, I have learned that the key to survival is just being honest. I have never understood why it's so hard for some people to be truthful. However, we should all learn to question anyone or anything that is not coming cross in an honest manner. Furthermore, once we do find someone that is truly honest we should hold on to that person with every ounce of love we can find.

In the following poem, "The Honest Apple", the story is told of a frustrated soul who finds himself eating alot of bad apples that discourage his spirit before he encounters the one good apple that embraces and loves his soul forever. It's a story of hope that there are true, honest souls out there, but we have to believe God will all allow our paths to cross with this person in the right way at the right time.

The Honest Apple
I was looking high and low for
The most honest apple I could find
Somehow all the rotten ones threw themselves
At me just to make me lose my mind

I was tired of trying so hard to
Balance everything in my midst
So I decided to search a deserted apple tree
With a promise life would be better than this

I sat under the apple tree waiting
For an honest apple to fall
Yet all of them seemed so far out of reach
That I felt I had hit the largest wall

Frustrated and confused I climbed this
Apple tree hoping to try out a few
Somehow I knew there had to be
Just one whose heart was really true

I took a bite of one apple that

Immediately gave me a bad taste
I could feel it had lived a life of getting others
To succumb to its deceptive ways

I then took another bite of an apple
That seemed sweet to the touch
Yet the aftertaste was so bitter I realized
This one was full of bad luck

So I moved a little further and grabbed
An apple that just felt good in my hands
Yet as soon as I touched it this one crumbled
Away as if it did not care to understand

I grabbed another apple and
Bit right into its core
Yet there was nothing solid to sustain
My spirit so it left me hungry for more

I saw another apple that I tried
To lift close to my mouth
But the bugs inside of it had damaged its
Sweetness that I had no choice but to throw it out

I took another chance taking bite of
Another apple that seemed safe to try
When I took a bite it just did not fulfill
Me so I kept asking myself why

After all the bad apples that I let play

Games with my heart and soul
I finally found the one honest apple shining in front
Of me with such kindness I would never let it go

Chapter 31 - The Heartfelt Connection

Life is truly all about connections with family, friends, co-workers, and even mere acquaintances. We go through this life feeling the need to connect with our loved ones in very special ways. However, we also run across some not so good souls whose intentions may end up hurting us rather than helping us feel good.

After all the hurt, sometimes in life there comes what I call a magical kind of connection of the heart that cannot be explained or even understood at times. We meet someone special whose eyes of beauty and charm lock with our own and suddenly we become drawn to this person with true beauty and grace.

The following poem, "The Heartfelt Connection", is all about finding that one person whose soul resonates in true love and harmony with our own. Sometimes we experience different relationships with others so we can one day find the one person who loves us unconditionally with the kind of spiritual love that will sustain us in the best and worst of times.

The Heartfelt Connection
I tried all my life to figure
Out what it all means
Why some people come and go
And others remain behind the scenes

There are some people who never
Quite understand who we are
Because all they want is to see
How they can tear us apart

Maybe some people think they can
Change us into what they need
Yet really all the heart wants is to be
Loved and cherished without deceit

Sometimes people think they
Know for us what is best
When our weary souls long for peaceful
Words to give us a chance to rest

There are times people walk onto our
Paths who really don't give us hope

We find ourselves broken once again
And struggling once more to really cope

Then along comes a special person
God sends to let us know love is real
It's like experiencing a paradise of
Beautiful dreams that is so good to feel

The heart wants what it wants in a person
That loves us no matter what
All the past hurts don't matter because this one
Learned what love is and what it is not

When the right person loves us it is like
Walking in a field of colorful flowers
Each flower echoes a symphony of happiness
Protected by love's magical powers

A true kindred spirit in life loves us
And encourages us to never give up
This one has the kind of heart you know
Through everything you can trust

A soulmate stays in love with every fiber
Of our spirit regardless of what we do
This special soul knows exactly how to share
A positive energy that is healthy and true

The spiritual connection between two hearts
Is an amazing love story we all wish to find

Then one day we look up and see it
Has been right before us all this time

Chapter 32 - The Angel and the Streets of Gold

It is very true that I find myself dreaming quite often of what life would be like on the other side to really connect with loved ones who have crossed over. As hard as this life can be, I know that there will not be any suffering when I go to Heaven. I have had many visions of what the other side will look like when it is my time.

Because I often dream of living in true spiritual paradise, I think about what it would be like to live among the angels and to be able to help those in this life struggling to make it from one day to the next. Sometimes I have felt how awesome it would be just to be a true guardian angel to help others in ways that this life here on earth often restricts.

The following poem, "The Angels and The Streets of Gold",

is all about how one soul's life is destined to be cut short so she can cross over to the other side. Even though this soul finds herself questioning why she had to go so soon, she meets a special angel who walks with her all throughout Heaven. With the guidance of this angel, she learns that she can now help others from a different place where true spiritual healing never dies.

The Angel and The Streets of Gold

In the blink of an eye everything
In my life suddenly went dark
It was as if someone had taken the
Sharpest knife and ran it right into my heart

Confused and not sure what
I was really meant to do
I felt a spiritual presence leading me away
From this world into a paradise that seemed true

I looked down and saw so many people standing
Around me wondering why God took me so soon
Even I was wondering why I had to leave my family
And a life in which I felt so in tune

Yet an angel came right up
Beside me and took me by the hand
She whispered sometimes you have to let go
And know a different life awaits you so try to understand

I walked hand in hand with this angel as she
Told me what I could teach this world
She whispered make sure you send others good energy
So they know they are loved when they feel hurt

As I kept walking these streets of gold the angel said
Send back an energy to give people peace
I felt as unbalanced as this world was maybe
I could help others find a calm release

The further we walked she told me to send
Whispers of joy to hearts feeling broken
I knew there were so many around me lost in a world
Of angry words that had been misspoken

In the midst of our walk a white dove flew
Right past me as if to give me hope
The angel cried send back an energy of strength
To give those who are lost the ability to cope

A little further down the streets of gold I could
Not help but think I would miss the life I had
The angel just squeezed my hand harder to
Let me know I would no longer feel sad

I realized as short as my life had been that
There had to be a reason God took me to this place
The angel said you have to know you are an angel now
Meant to reassure others with your caring ways

As I stood hand in hand with my angelic friend
At the edge of Heaven I knew I had no reason to cry
Now my spiritual energy could reach the lives
Of struggling souls to know it is ok to ask why

The day I reached the streets of gold was a change
In my fate I truly did not expect
The angel walked away telling me to remind others
Love is the best feeling they should not forget

I got down on my knees in Heaven that day asking
God to let my loving spirit protect those left behind
Now I could teach others through my energies
To love each other relentlessly until it is their time

Chapter 33 - Walking in the Shadows

Whether we realize it or not we all have shadows around us of many people, places, and things that often we neglect to really see due to the busy nature of our lives. For most of my life I have always felt there were shadows of struggle following me closely making me feel it was too hard for me to catch a break when I needed it most. I guess you could say I have always been the underdog with a big heart. My life has been blessed, but it has not been easy to say the least.

For as long as I can remember, I have felt shadows of difficulty wanting to suffocate the very goodness out of my heart and soul. It is almost like I always thought I was on the outside looking in watching everyone else while I tried to figure out why I had to always come up with the short end of the stick so many times. However, instead of having a self-proclaimed pity party in my life, I have learned to take the shadows of hardship and turn them into some of the greatest lessons God has ever taught me. I accepted a long time ago that my present struggles are just preparing me for an even greater existence when I make it to Heaven.

In the following poem, "Walking in the Shadows", the person in this narrative poem has suffered alot in life, yet he or she knows that when his or her time is over in this life, a much better story awaits him or her on the other side. Despite the problems we all face, there is truly hope that we grow stronger through adversity and will be spiritually rewarded one day for our perseverance.

Walking in the Shadows

I was walking in the shadows
Of a life I could no longer take
It seemed the life I was living had become
What I considered a tragic mistake

Everyone always thought I was the life
Of the party but they don't know my pain inside
I have been in the shadow of other people's success
And could not understand why

The more I walked the more the shadows of
Lost dreams seemed to pull me off track
I know everyone said hang in there but
I could not help but look back

I thought of all the times I tried to be
What everyone else thought was best
Yet despite my happy façade I felt my spirit was
Always undergoing some challenging test

As the years of my life have passed by I thought
Maybe I would not be chasing so many dreams
I figured at some point everything would come
Together but life is never what it seems

Sometimes the shadows before me cast
A reflection of all I ever wanted to be
But mostly they served to be a reminder of
How I let this world get the best of me

I have tried to catch the shadows of doubt to try
And get them to see my point of view
Yet they seem to grow longer and out of my reach
Like a lost child who struggles in school

Sometimes I wonder why the shadows of life
Have always cast an unhappy glow on my soul
As hard as it is I always tried hard to feel good
Even when I would rather just let go

Every direction I turn shadows of broken promises
And false hopes haunt my mind
In my weary spirit all I can do is hope I can discover
What is loyal and true before I run out of time

Over and over again I keep chasing these shadows
Of a life that intensifies my anxiety
And I laugh within myself because I know that
Feeling misguided has become my reality

I have spent my whole life walking in the shadows
And felt my time in this world had come to an end
In my final hours I left this world hoping
In the afterlife a better life would begin

Chapter 34 - Spiritual Protection in the Midst of a Seagull Collection

It's funny but true that I always thought that if I were to come back as another creature of human nature it would be as a seagull because I love the beach, and I love the freedom these birds have to go to any coastal waters in sight. Since I always thought the only way to see a seagull was to go to the beach, I was rather surprised when I walked outside an exercise facility in my hometown to look up and see a flock of seagulls decorating the North Carolina mountain sky! I had to do a double take at first to make sure what I was seeing was really before my eyes. However, I could feel there was something really different about these seagulls in the mountains.

I believe that when we die we do cross over into the spirit world, and I also believe that our loved ones on the other side have this amazing ability to transform into beautiful creatures of nature. With that said, the very day I saw these beautiful seagulls flying in such peaceful harmony, I could not help but think it was the spirits of those crossed over wanting to spread their peace and love over those who were lucky enough like me to see and feel their presence. It just so happened to be a day when I was really feeling down and in need of some encouragement.

In the following poem, "Spiritual Protection in the Midst of a Seagull Collection", the story is inspired by my own special experience in the mountains seeing these seagulls. It is a story of hope because sometimes in the moments when we need to know someone cares we never know when any beautiful force of nature could catch us by surprise to comfort us in our time and need of true healing.

Spiritual Protection in the Midst of a Seagull Collection

From the mysteries of the coastal waters
I could not believe my eyes
That in the high country of great hopes
A flock of seagulls caught me by surprise

My heart had been so heavy and sad for
All the souls that had lived and died
Yet these seagulls reminded me to see
The good despite all my unanswered whys

I watched each lovely white bird fly

With such elegance and grace
They flew in sync to let me know those
Who died were at peace in many ways

I still wanted to cry but I knew in my heart
They each wanted me to be strong
The souls who had crossed over now became
Seagulls of peace like the comfort of a good love song

I kept thinking to myself that each seagull
Had a special story to tell
When they walked the world as humans
Times were good but then at times life was a living hell

I watched each seagull closely and could feel
Each soul I knew who had crossed my path
It was as if these birds said you cannot give up
No matter how much your spirit is under attack

Confused and uncertain if I had the strength
To keep going through the motions
The seagulls shifted their flight as if to say keep the faith
And you will find peace with your emotions

Fighting the urge myself to wonder why
Their lives had to be taken so soon
Each one flew right past me as if their energies
Of hope were keeping my soul spiritually intune

In my heart I questioned them and asked if they were

Upset to have their lives end without warning
The gentle breeze I felt from their delicate wings
Let me know they were now at peace every morning

In a spirit of complete wonder I was so amazed
These seagulls flew so close by each other's side
They said you have to keep making the
Most of your own life until it is your time

With some hesitation I was not sure how much longer
I could pretend all in my world was great
Yet the spiritual protection I found in the midst
Of a seagull collection reassured me all would be ok

Chapter 35 - The Rearview Mirror and the Destined Road

We all have that tendency to look back when we know we really need to look forward. I think change is probably one of the hardest things for any of us to truly fulfill. We get scared thinking we may be making the wrong move when in all actuality it is the best thing we could ever do.

I have wasted alot of time in my own life looking in the rearview mirror wondering why I did this or that or wondering if I should have stayed involved in certain situations. As I have gotten older, I have come to realize that life is way too short to have regrets. I do believe that every situation we face is meant to teach us something, and once that lesson has been learned then we must take the lesson and move forward in our lives in the best ways possible.

The following poem, "The Rearview Mirror and the Destined Road", is all about breaking the unhealthy cycle of looking back with regret and replacing it with a new mindset that better and happier roads await us all. Even if the past was not good, there is always a much brighter future awaiting us all. We all just have to have hope that no matter what has happened we can face new roads with greater joy and enthusiasm.

The Rearview Mirror and the Destined Road

I decided to take a drive down a new road
Not knowing where it would lead
Yet I found myself looking back in my
Rearview mirror at a life no longer good for me

I could see images in the mirror of all
The times I gave without appreciation
Even though I did not see it at the time
I was astounded at the level of humiliation

I thought maybe this new road did not
Seem that bad after all
When I glanced in the rearview mirror
I caught myself many times with my back against the wall

With some fear I felt I needed to keep driving
This new road because I needed a change
Then I took another look in the rearview mirror
And was sad at the times I felt so ashamed

145

The road before me seemed quite interesting
For me to keep driving down
Yet my eyes kept racing back to the
Rearview mirror before I escaped my present town

I could feel the lure of this road motivating me
To keep driving to see what was in store
When I looked again in the rearview mirror
I saw the life I left behind was not meant for me anymore

I saw the sun breaking through the clouds as
I kept driving to a new destination
When I looked back in the rearview mirror
I could feel how happy I was to leave all my desperation

I saw some detours on this new road before me
But I felt this road was the right one for me
I realized looking back in the rearview mirror
Would just reinforce all my past misery

I liked the fact I was in control now of a new destiny
With the road of hope under my wheels
After looking into the rearview mirror
The beautiful landmarks I passed let me know how love feels

I was driving for hours on end but the lure of
A brand new adventure kept me feeling strong
When I glanced at the rearview mirror I realized
Its purpose helped me let go so I could move on

With the destined road before me leading to a life
That would help me find true happiness
I was now moving forward away from the rearview mirror
To a new life of eternal love and kindness

Chapter 36 - Games Energy Vampires Play

If there are two words I have come to know well in my lifetime it would be "energy vampire". It took me a long time to understand exactly how an energy vampire affects one's heart and soul. However, I came to discover through many draining encounters just how frustrating these people can really be.

The question now becomes how can we spot those pesky energy vampires? Well, think about it in the following ways. When we find ourselves feeling totally exhausted and pushed around by someone who thinks he or she knows what is best for us, it is more than likely we have encountered an energy vampire. If we find ourselves being subjected to constant communication from someone who is always about his or her own agenda and rarely asks us about our own, then we have met up with an energy vampire. If we discover that we feel totally violated from the inside out thinking we could trust someone who really just wanted to break our spirits in half, then we have encountered an energy vampire. Therefore, it is so important to recognize the signs.

The following poem, "Games Energy Vampires Play", is all about the sly and deceptive ways in which energy vampires work. They have this uncanny way of making us all feel that we are there to serve their needs, yet as I have learned this is a case where we all need to be strong and protect our energy from being endangered.

Games Energy Vampires Play

Once upon time in a land
That was very close to home
I had become the prisoner of many different
Energy vampires whose hearts had grown cold

I tried and tried to be a good friend to them
So I could help these vampires find their way
They thought playing with the hands of fate would
Make them superior to me with each passing day

Energy vampires as clever as they are kept telling me
What would keep me in their midst
Yet their intentions were so deceptive that
It is no wonder my spirit was ready to quit

I thought maybe acts of kindness would
Turn their false fronts around
But no matter what I did they each found a way
To lie right to my face despite the truth I found

It has amazed me how certain energy vampires
Seem to know how to make me cry
By the time one of my encounters was over
With them I often wondered why should I try

The good within me pushed me to give
My energy vampires the benefit of the doubt
Yet despite their friendly facade I felt getting away
From their games was my only way out

Some people told me maybe I was sent to
Help the energy vampires face the truth
But the sad thing is I found myself once again
Disillusioned by their games and feeling like a fool

I prayed and asked God to help me find a way
To deal with this huge strain on my soul
Everyday despite the strength I was given
I felt the energy vampires would not let me go

Many times I felt like maybe I could just
Run away without looking back
Yet the energy vampires keep me chained
To their side though their hearts were off track

Eventually I felt like sometimes being good
To those who hurt you is not a bad deed
But we all have our limits for those feeding
Off our souls with their tricks and deceit

Oh the games people play with our hearts
And minds is one where nobody truly wins
The energy vampires keep on draining us innocent souls
Hoping to keep us as their only friends

Chapter 37 - Confusion and Disillusion that Led to Something Soothing

There are times in this life when we all feel totally confused and disillusioned. Sometimes it can seem that we are never going to be successful achieving our dreams when there are so many things trying to steer us in unhealthy directions. I know because I have spent so much of my life feeling that I had to please other people in order to embrace a better and happier life for myself. The end result though for me was that the more I tried to please everyone else, the more I ended up feeling more confused and disillusioned about the path I was meant to travel.

At this point in my life's journey, I have come to realize that it is so much better to go with the flow and trust that everything that happens is for a reason. We may not always understand why certain things happen, and it may discourage us to try and figure out all the answers, and that is totally ok.

The more we sometimes try to figure things out, the more confused and disillusioned we can become. Therefore, I feel it is best to take life one day at a time and make the best of each moment because eventually things will get better.

The following poem, "Confusion and Disillusion that Led to Something Soothing", is all about working through the misleading times of life to embrace true hope that awaits us all no matter what our struggles may be.

Confusion and Disillusion that Led to Something Soothing
I was sitting in front of an ocean
Far away from all I had known
I was begging God to help me break away
From a life that had grown so cold

The waves kept crashing on the shore yet
The confusion in my mind would never stop
I just looked up to the Heavens and asked God
When it would be my turn to come out on top

The confusing side of my mind said it would be
Easier if I stayed right where things seemed safe
Yet when I looked out over the ocean I could feel
The waves crashing harder with such rage

I then reasoned that maybe I could just start fresh
And not care what everyone thought

153

I noticed a seagull flew right past me with such peace
I could not imagine staying distraught

I decided to take a walk hoping God would
Send me a sign of what I was meant to do
All the confusion in my soul kept me trapped too long
To a life that was unhealthy and untrue

My mind was filled with memories of
All the times I had been treated so badly
The moments of disillusion from my past
Reminded me of how often I was misled so sadly

There was a true tug of war raging within saying
Should I stay to please others or should I leave
The hopeful side of my heart said it is time to let go
And live a life of freedom just meant for me

The further I walked down this sandy shore
I could feel confusion trying to stop my direction
Yet the heart of my very being said there's nothing to fear
Because love awaits you without rejection

I felt I was playing a mental game of ping pong
Weighing out what God wanted for my life
He sent a warm breeze to embrace my struggling spirit
To say trust me it will all turn out all right

I could feel the confusion of my past and disillusion
Of false friends trying to get me to turn back yet the new

direction
Where I was heading filled me with hope
As I knew I was finally on the right track

As my adventure on a sandy shore of a better life
Kept pushing me to a fresh destiny
I was greeted by a kindred spirit who after
All the confusion and disillusion, loved me honestly

Chapter 38 - The Magic Drink Called Peace of Mind

If there is one thing I feel we all truly strive for in each of our lives, it would be the gift of peace of mind. So many of us search for so many ways to find peace that we often just settle for a temporary fix that often leaves us feeling more unsettled wanting something more and something more fulfilling.

In my own life's journey, I have tried and done many things thinking it would bring me peace. However, the things I thought would make me feel at ease really just were a seductive trap of deception that ended up leaving me more frustrated and broken from the inside out. It's sad that there are so many people or things that try to make us think we can find peace if we just give in to their alluring charms. However, I have discovered that true peace only comes from

God, and He gives us the inner peace we need that will sustain us through our struggles through the best and worst of times.

The following poem, "The Magic Drink Called Peace of Mind", illustrates one person's failed attempts to find peace in the wrong places. However, eventually this person discovers the inner peace he or she is seeking that leads to more beautiful and wonderful discoveries that are no longer covered by deceitful disguises.

The Magic Drink Called Peace of Mind

Something told me there were some drinks
Not too good for my soul
Yet I tried the drink of pleasing everyone
But it frustrated me until I felt led to let it go

In many ways I thought I could try a drink
That would just fill me with such satisfaction
Yet the more I let it soak my body within the more
I was repulsed by its false attraction

I tried another drink that made me feel dizzy
As if I just wanted to sleep and not wake up
The harder I tried to run away from my present fears
The more I felt my hopeful spirit was stuck

I went searching every store for a drink that
Could somehow soothe my restless heart

Yet the drinks that kept me on a high brought me down
Quite fast as if my world kept falling apart

So I found a cup of coffee that I felt
Would warm up my cold spirit within
Yet the moment I took a drink it was so hot
That it burned my heart desperate to begin again

I was feeling quite discouraged as if all
The drinks I tried just let me down
But a still small spiritual voice whispered don't
Give up just yet because hope is to be found

With a feeling of courage in my soul I decided
To keep looking for a new kind of drink
This time I felt I needed to grab one with
A more peaceful edge that would make me think

In my mind I visualized a sunrise lingering above the horizon
With such beauty I felt all would be fine
Despite all my problems drinking in its radiance
Convinced me everything would work out in time

Then my mind traveled to a meadow of colorful flowers
Whose charm made me feel at ease
With every breath I found myself drinking in the
Power of their kindness putting an end to my misery

I then imagined I was sailing away from home
On an ocean to embrace a new start in life drinking in the

Smell of the saltwater and a warm, gentle breeze helped
Me not give up without a fight

My mind then escaped to an island where the only comfort
I had was my desire to find some balance
The precious drink of solitude caressed my spirit saying
Keep the faith and you will survive the malice

In a few moments my mind kept thinking of all times
Past where I felt nothing could quench my thirst
Yet the thoughts of a drink built on serene taste
Kept me putting my heartfelt needs first

After all the good and bad drinks I have had during
My time in this phase of my existence
The magic drink called peace of mind is where my
Heart and soul was able to overcome all resistance

Chapter 39 - The Disease Called Emotional Fatigue

Sometimes I find myself just getting tired of being tired. It seems I find myself going through the motions of life pretending everything is great on the outside when my spirit feels totally worn out on the inside. There are moments that it feels I am just going from one thing to the next with half a heart wondering what my purpose really is.

In fact, I think if we were all being totally honest with ourselves, we would admit that we go through the motions of life pretending all is well when in all actuality we are very exhausted. Let's face it. Life is very draining and hard for all of us. We can get so busy doing so many things that we neglect what our hearts and souls want most which is just to take a break sometimes and find the time to rest to get a better handle on our problems.

The following poem, "The Disease Called Emotional Fatigue", is all about trying to overcome the stress life's struggles can often cause us when we feel so overwhelmed and discouraged. Even though it's normal to get tired, I have discovered that it is very important to take some time out to give our hearts and souls a break from unrelenting chaos and stress and just find healthy ways to rejuvenate our hearts and minds.

The Disease Called Emotional Fatigue
I was suffering from an illness that kept
My heart trapped in a sea of repression
My soul never understood why I was
So tired of reliving life's most challenging lessons

I decided to take a trip within myself in
The hopes I could understand what was wrong
I saw a woman trying to rescue her dying spirit
From a life of hope that was almost gone

There were moments I saw how much I
Gave of myself and got very little in return
It was no wonder I felt like I could barely breathe
Feeling like I was the one always getting burned

My mind was brought back to the past to times
When I just kept giving until I had nothing left

Yet somehow I figured out that I needed to let go
Of what was not working so I could quit getting upset

The cycles of pain seemed to keep playing
Themselves out over and over again in my mind
My restless soul was sick and tired of getting hurt
In many different ways all the time

I tried to look deeper within myself to understand
What had caused my spirit to fail
What I found was a part of me remained broken
From unfulfilled dreams keeping me feeling unwell

Somewhere in all my soul searching I felt I needed
To understand why I always felt so stressed
My life felt like a roller coaster at times leaving
My emotions tossed about in a sea of unrest

I wanted to find a way to find my happy self again
Because the sadness of life was hard to ignore
Yet I knew living with half a heart was no way
To live a life I was so ready to throw out the door

Sometimes I look in the mirror and really do
Not know who I am supposed to be at all
What I do know is I find myself on the brink
Of a high mountain on the verge of a great fall

I thought taking a few deep breaths might bring
Back the vitality of my soul once again

Despite my past and present setbacks
I knew the old me still had a spirit determined to win

It's funny how there are some things simple
Doctor's orders and medicine is not able to fix
This disease called emotional fatigue is an ailment
I hope my heart and soul eventually can resist

Chapter 40 - The Suitcase Solution

We have all experienced those times when we felt like just packing up a suitcase and getting far away from all the things in our lives that weigh us down. Just like so many of us, I have thought countless times when I was feeling truly discouraged that I needed to just pack up all my stuff and run away to another place and time. Even though I know you can't truly run away from your problems, I have learned that it's ok to escape the stress of tough times when needed.

I have learned that when I take time out from stressful situations I often can come back to them and solve my problems much easier as I have given myself the time and space needed to come to some positive resolutions. It is so much better to take time to figure things out than to make hasty decisions. In fact, every time I got away from some of my own problems, I found that once I returned back to reality I developed a stronger resolve to solve my issues in better, productive ways.

The following poem, "The Suitcase Solution", is all about escaping the stresses of life in such a way that we all can find hopeful outcomes to trying situations in the most effective ways possible. Running away does not solve problems, but it definitely gives us the ability to find better solutions to the issues causing us stress.

The Suitcase Solution

I decided to pack a suitcase with
Just what I needed to survive
Somehow I felt my life was far from
The way I thought it should be this time

I looked for a spiritual book to take
To help keep me strong
So I packed several with different messages
To be my soul's guiding light and forever hopeful song

I threw in my laptop hoping I could write
A new book where all my issues were addressed
In many ways I still felt a sense of unease
In my spirit in desperate need of rest

I threw in my gold cross necklace with
The hopes of finding some forever good luck

Somehow I knew I was destined to
Keep going and never give up

Then I threw in my charming stones of empathic protection
With faith nobody could break me down
From this point forward I now could run
Those manipulative souls way out of town

I threw just what clothes I needed to
Keep me warm and cool when needed
This time I was determined not to be victimized
By false games leaving my good heart feeling cheated

I packed my best comfortable shoes to help me
Stand strong just in case someone hurt me
My good friend karmic justice would guide
My journey and save me from any misery

Then I grabbed some snacks and a few sodas
To keep my eager spirit nourished
No matter how hungry I got I knew
Some trustworthy foods would keep me encouraged

With great satisfaction I took my suitcase
And threw it into the trunk of my car
I now felt God giving me the strength to
Keep going no matter the odds and no matter how far

I pushed the accelerator knowing the
Only way now was to push straight ahead

My suitcase and I knew it was time to break away
From my troubles and embrace a better life instead

With peaceful music playing on the radio bringing
Great satisfaction to my heart and soul
I discovered the suitcase solution was the cure
My weary spirit needed to move on and finally let go

Chapter 41 - Sleepwalking Through Time

I was always fascinated with the concept of sleepwalking. Most people identify sleepwalking as performing other activities without any conscious recollection of what you have done or said. I have always gotten this vision of someone who sleepwalks just aimlessly going from one room to another in a household without having any idea what he or she has done the next day.

When I think about sleepwalking, I came to see that in many ways we all have spent time sleepwalking though different areas of our lives. Maybe we did not perform sleepwalking in the ways it is defined, but we have all had times where we felt emotionally numb going through life has if our hearts and souls are frozen in pain. I think we have all had those times where we were physically present but emotionally a million miles away. Others try to make connections to us, but our hearts and minds seem to be lost in space and time.

The following poem, "Sleepwalking Through Time", is all about going through the motions of one's life, yet it contains the hopeful energy of knowing that eventually he or she will awaken to a life that is meaningful and happy after spending so much time feeling lost.

Sleepwalking Through Time

I was sleepwalking through life
As if nothing really mattered
All I could hear was chaos
And tons of unhealthy chatter

My mind said I know you
Are tired of giving so much
My heart said that is who you are
Even when you feel out of luck

I felt I had been sleepwalking through
Many moments in time
I found myself standing on the sidelines
Like a lost soul losing his mind

When I was a child I felt
Sleepwalking was such a fantasy

Now I find myself desperate to escape
Sleepwalking to free me from insanity

I toss and turn at night with anxious
Thoughts running in my head
Sometimes I feel maybe it would be best
If I just sleepwalk instead

Through all the chapters in my life
Where I felt I had learned a lesson
Sleepwalking just reminded me of how hard
It is to escape the demon of depression

It seems through sleepwalking I realized
How asleep I have really always been
In my search for true peace I just hope
To have a forever faithful friend

Sometimes I pretend to be happy just
To make others think I am ok
Yet my heart just wants to be free from
Sleepwalking so tomorrow will be a better day

Sleepwalking is an unwelcome journey
I never realized would become a reality
No wonder I find myself going through
The motions feeling unsure of my destiny

I find myself often sleepwalking
Through one dream to the next

It is no wonder I wake up feeling tired
With a spirit in dire need of rest

Sleepwalking through life has become
A bad hobby I did not mean to pursue
I hope and pray God gives me the strength
To wake up to a life that's honestly true

Chapter 42 - Karmic Justice and All Those Pesky Flies

One of my favorite words has always been karma as I love the concept that we truly reap what we sow in this life. It has always amazed me how so many people can go through this life hurting other people without getting the proper repercussions. It has further upset me to see innocent people hurt at the hands of others who only seem to care about themselves rather than anyone else.

We all have had times when we were unfairly treated by someone or something that maybe seemed quite innocent yet turned out to be very destructive to our hearts and souls. I have definitely been wronged just like so many of us have, but I have learned that it's best to not get revenge and just let God take care of it. Eventually those who have wronged us will have to own up to what they did. If it does not happen in this life, it will surely happen in the one to come. In the meantime, we just have to not let the struggles of this life get the better of us and know that hope is on our side.

The following poem, "Karmic Justice and All Those Pesky Flies", is all about standing strong in the midst of difficult circumstances and people and not letting anyone or anything break us down. It is a poem of knowing eventually everything will work out ok as long as we don't lose hope in the beauty of true justice.

Karmic Justice and All Those Pesky Flies

I was searching through the map
Of life trying to figure out my destiny
I was so tired of letting this
Crazy world get the best of me

I decided it was time to take a journey
Into a deeper part of my soul
And with this travel I knew it was time
To let all those pesky flies around me finally go

I fell right into the desert where one fly
Wanted to keep me feeling totally lost
This one just persisted but I walked away
Knowing the loss was well worth the cost

I then was thrust right into raging waters

Where it was all I could do to stay afloat
The fly swarming around my head was enough
For me to swim faster to the quickest life boat

In just a few seconds I landed on
A mountain top not sure of what to do
Then this pesky fly who haunted my mind
I released without feeling like such a fool

In a matter of minutes I found myself walking
A tightrope over the highest valley I could find
Despite the pesky fly around me I was eager
To break free from my pain for good this time

I then jumped into a kayak fighting against the
Unpredictable ocean waters in the current of life
Even though another pesky fly tried to tempt me
I just smiled at him and waved goodbye

Without a moment to figure out where
I was headed on my next adventurous stop
I chased away another pesky fly as I embraced
A new world knowing I would finally come out on top

I kept spinning the globe of change hoping
It would land in a place of forever good luck
The pesky flies spinning around me eventually
Gave up because they knew I would not stay stuck

I felt my life had taught me great lessons

Regardless of the pesky flies always in my way
Every time they interfered in my happiness
I was determined to embrace a brand new day

As the chapters of my life began to fly right past me
I decided I could now breathe a sigh of peace
Because the powers of karmic justice made sure
Those pesky flies left my side with a calm release

Chapter 43 - The Secret to Happiness

Happiness is definitely something I feel we all spend our entire lives trying to find. It is as if we long for the days when we can finally put an end to our sadness and embrace a lifetime of sheer bliss. We all think that maybe something or someone can make us happy. Even though that may very well be true at times, I have learned that we really cannot depend on other people or material possessions to make us happy all the time.

After years of looking to others to help me feel good about myself, I realized very quickly that I was wrong to expect that someone else could give me the validation I so wanted. I have spent so much of my life trying to make everyone else happy that I spent so many years feeling lost in a wilderness of regret. Even though I still struggle with trying to please others at times, I can honestly say I finally learned that I must have faith in myself and know that I do not have to be at the mercy of other peoples' expectations and that it is ok to honor what feels good to me no matter what someone else thinks.

The following poem, "The Secret to Happiness", tells the story of a soul who dreams he or she goes to Heaven searching for the secret to happiness only to find a series of angels who share their spiritual views on what it takes to have true joy throughout the journey of our lives.

The Secret to Happiness

In the midst of a hopeful dream
I searched for the secret to a happy life
I was not sure which way to look
But I knew I had to keep living right

I took a trip to Heaven and asked God if
He could help me find a smile that would last
He just led me to a group of angels to help
Me learn to let go of my hurtful past

I walked around the streets of gold hoping
The angels could give me a clue
I could hear them talking among themselves
Hoping I would quit being so confused

In my quest for the secret to happiness
I asked one angel why it was hard to feel so good

He just grinned and said I learned early
On to just do the best I could

Then I walked a little further and asked
Another angel what made her laugh
She said I know now I have to keep the faith
And learn to quit looking back

Eager for another answer to help me find
A solution to find a joy that I could trust
An angel walked right beside me and gave me
A nice charm to bring me better luck

I wanted to learn more about the
Waves of happiness so few ever find
Some angel just whispered and said you must
Take care of yourself this time

I wandered around for hours hoping to
Catch a glimpse of a rainbow in the clouds
One friendly angel said trust your instincts and
The happiness you seek will be yours without a doubt

I searched high and low for a place where
Happiness and I could finally cross paths forever
All the angels said our love for your soul will
Bring you eternal joy you can always treasure

Back home I looked everywhere for the opportunity
To be happy in a world marked with pain

One angel finally whispered look within yourself
To find happy seeds that can grow without shame

As I woke up one morning I was amazed at the
Dream that had taught me so much
With spiritual insight I learned the secret to happiness
Is caring about yourself without giving up

Chapter 44 - The Brevity of Life

It would be so nice if we could all just go through life without a care or worry in the world and live in a universe where there is no pain or suffering. It would be so nice if we could just wake up everyday to the sun shining so brightly that we think we will be forever in the light. It would be so nice if everyone in the world was truly at peace so we could live in a harmonious universe.

As much as we all can dream of a perfect existence, the truth is there are lots of hardships and struggles in this world, and none of us are immune from those inevitable dark times that often bring stress to our lives. Someway and somehow we all are eventually faced with trying times that can either make us or break us.

The following poem, "The Brevity of Life", is all about one

soul's journey who is led by God into the wilderness of despair frustrated with his or her life and wondering why me? This narrative poem is a lesson to all of us that life really is short. Therefore, no matter what comes our way we must learn through our struggles and embrace the fact that pain gives us strength to hold onto hope during our most challenging battles in this life.

The Brevity of Life

God grabbed me by the hand
And said come take a walk with me
He made sure I knew it was time
To learn what life should truly be

He took me through a forest
That was so dark and dreary
I felt sick to my stomach because
I knew I was already weak and weary

God said look around and
Tell me what you really feel
I gasped for breath and said I know in life
There has to be more hope that is real

I decided to look around and was
Not sure where God had gone
He whispered you have to feel lost sometimes
To understand why the rights went wrong

I kept walking aimlessly around
Looking for all the right signs
Yet all I could see were the dark clouds
Keeping the sun from coming out this time

Somewhere in the middle of this forest
I begged God to somehow give me a break
Through the foggy air I could hear Him whisper
Life is not easy but it's ok to make mistakes

I was confused as to what God wanted me
To learn about a life I no longer wanted
All I could see was the grey mist of despair
Keeping my spirit feeling haunted

I found myself wandering around the forest
Of questions in a state of utter confusion
Then God sent a warm, gentle breeze and a ray
Of sunshine to say keep the faith through all illusion

Tired of all the drama of troubling voices
That kept my head constantly spinning
I got down on my knees praying God would
Show mercy on my spirit needing a new beginning

During the maze of uncertain twists and turns
God wanted to me to feel and understand
I realized sometimes you have to be strong
In order to conquer the challenging tasks at hand

While enduring the forest of trying times
That strengthened my search for hope
God taught me the brevity of life is something
To be treasured no matter how hard it is to cope

Chapter 45 - The Test of Time

The truth is we all wish we just had more time. We wish we had more time to visit family and friends. We wish we had time to take more of a break from work. We wish we had more money. We wish we had more time to take a vacation that lasts much longer than a few days. We wish we could just do what we want when we want. The wish list goes on and on for so many of us if we just had more time.

I can honestly say that I have wasted alot of my own time in this life wondering what my purpose is and why God made me to feel so different than other people. Throughout my lifetime, I have always felt like I did not fit in with anyone as I have always been a free spirit often feeling misunderstood by those who maybe thought silently to themselves why does she not just do this or that. The truth is maybe I never was really misunderstood because maybe just maybe what I thought others were thinking about me was not really the case at all.

If I have come to learn anything in my adult life, it is that I finally accepted that it is ok to take the time to just be true to myself. I have wished more times than I can count that I could go ahead and cross over to the other side as I have felt often like a lost spiritual soul just waiting to get back to God.

As hard as this life has been for me, I finally realized as the following poem, "The Test of Time", suggests that God wants us all to make the most of everyday He has given us no matter how challenging it may be. It is true that time flies, but it is even more true that God gives us the ability to make our lives something special as we have this one chance to keep on trying until we get it right.

The Test of Time

I was walking in circles looking
For a way to the other side
God said you have to endure all the tests
Here in this life before it is your time

I was desperate to escape into
A new world where there was no pain
God said all the tests I have planned for you
Will challenge your good name

I prayed and asked him to

185

Set my imprisoned spirit free
God said just keep the faith and
One day you will have no misery

I looked around and wondered
If my life would always be so chaotic
The lure of the other side had a
Spiritual charm my heart found so hypnotic

I was glad I could learn that this life was just
A stop until a better way could occur
God said a better day will come where
Your spirit will always be free to learn

There are times I don't understand why
I can't escape to the other side right now
God said you must grow stronger and
Keep the faith it will work out somehow

I know life is hard but I also know
The test of time is not giving up
God promised to protect me forever
With the best kind of spiritual luck

I smile now knowing all
Will work out in the end
Now I know I am not alone but in
The company of a much spiritual friend

Thank you God for giving me hope to know

Life will be a place of peace before too long
The test of time is keeping my spirits up
Like the pleasure of a good love song

The test of time is a mystery
But I hope I always understand
God will never let me go and make sure
He keeps holding my hand

Chapter 46 - Swimming Upstream In the Midst of Hopeful Dreams

One my of favorite expressions has always been that I always felt like I was swimming upstream. It seemed that if something difficult happened, it was bound and determined to come my way. There have been countless times I looked around in my life and saw everyone else who seemed to have everything going their way, and then I thought well there is me, this frustrated soul so desperately wanting a good break in her life.

After waking up from a lifetime of feeling frustrated that the rough waters of this life were always beating me up, I finally realized that life is truly what we make it. I could have been that girl who always felt the victim of bad circumstances or bad choices or I could be that girl who made the choice to rise above her struggles and meet her challenges head on. Rather than playing the victim, I discovered the best choice for me was embracing my struggles knowing with God's help I could come out much stronger on the other side.

The following poem, "Swimming Upstream in the Midst Of Hopeful Dreams", is all about not being afraid to face your problems no matter how difficult they may be. Our first instinct is usually to run away from our problems because maybe it will be too much to deal with them. However, swimming upstream against the current of life is what makes us strong enough to overcome the most raging waters of challenges that try to break us down so we can find peace during our pain.

Swimming Upstream In the Midst of Hopeful Dreams

Life and I had been struggling
Over how to win the fight
Yet I was thrown into a constant raging river
Where I had to struggle with all my might

The harsh winds of pain knocked me
Right into the waters of despair
Yet I knew God had a purpose to keep
The faith that He would always care

The current of the river was so fierce
I felt how can I keep swimming

All I could think about were my thoughts
On how to survive were never-ending

In the middle of this crazy river
We often called life
I knew I had to keep swimming
And believe everything would be all right

The harder I swam against the current of conformity
The more fierce the water became
But I had worked so hard to be so true I did
Not want the problems to consume my good name

My body kept hitting one hard rock after the other
As I swam with courage in the river of tribulation
As tired as I was I knew I had to keep going
Despite all my sadness and frustration

Dark voices in my head kept trying to tell me
My life was worth nothing at all
Yet I had to believe there was still good in this life
Without feeling I was always hitting a brick wall

The rains came down hard on me as I
Kept swimming hoping to reach my dreams
There were black birds flying above me whose
Good intentions were not what they seemed

The once blue clouds became gray with thunder
And lightening kept raging above me

As I kept swimming, I wondered if the angels of hope
Would help me overcome this unforeseen misery

It felt as if I was swimming in a river where
The harsh currents kept getting rougher
Yet the force at which it weakened my spirit
Reminded me that I had to keep getting tougher

Swimming upstream is truly a struggle
I have endured for far too long
But I keep the faith God has a plan in my spiritual destiny
To keep my heart and soul strong

Chapter 47 - The Imprisoned Castle and the Butterfly of Freedom

In so many different avenues of our lives, we often find ourselves trapped under circumstances that can be so hard to control or manage. It can seem that the walls of hardship are closing in around us all when we strive to break free from the confinement of despair and stress. Sometimes it can seem that nobody really understands the very essence of our being as we strive to find a softer place for our wounded spirits to land.

Life for all of us can test us so much that we often are not sure where to turn or what to do. Sometimes the worries that often plague our souls can keep us forever imprisoned in a prison of insecurity that so many of us fall victim to. In the midst of our frustrations, sometimes we all just need to know that there is someone or something out there that truly cares about each of us for who we are and what we hope for.

In the following poem, "The Imprisoned Castle and the Butterfly of Freedom", the story is told of a lost soul feeling so disillusioned that he or she just longs to enjoy the simple freedoms of life and luckily discovers that a much needed true friend is divinely sent to help him or her find true joy.

The Imprisoned Castle and the Butterfly of Freedom

Once upon a time in what appeared
To be a land full of great dreams
There lived a princess so lovely whose life
With the prince was not what it seemed

On the outside of this castle life
Was charming and full of great wit
Yet on the inside there was a desperate princess
Who was fed up and ready to quit

Everyone thought they knew that her life
Was everything they had ever wanted
Yet on the inside she constantly felt trapped
By a life of pain keeping her feeling haunted

She wandered around her castle for
Countless hours wondering how to break free
Then spent much time asking God to
Release her from all her misery

After all her distress and despair she saw a
Yellow butterfly flapping its wings so peacefully
She wondered if it had the key to free
Her spirit in a way much more easily

She opened her window inviting this special little creature
Into a home that had grown cold
As she reached out her weary hands she felt
A strength within its little body encouraging her to be bold

This butterfly seemed to have a way of making
Her feel that life would get much better
The way it flapped its wings with courage
Made her feel she would endure the stormy weather

As she watched the butterfly fly with grace
Around her room in a spirit of determination
What once made her feel trapped within
Started to turn into a feeling of true exhilaration

She was in such awe of this butterfly who was
Not afraid to fly in the midst of bad times
Something about the way it soared with peace
Made her feel God was sending her a sign

She whispered to this butterfly and asked him
To help her escape a life she could no longer bear
The sweet butterfly flew around her in circles
Until she became like him with a new spirit to care

From that moment on the two butterflies flew
Out of that dark castle to meadows of nice flowers
They loved each other always knowing their life
Was now protected with great spiritual powers

Chapter 48 - The Mystery Mailbox

A mailbox is often something we take for granted because most of us check it everyday bombarded by bills or other junk mail that rarely makes a difference in how we feel or think. In the day to day routine of our lives, we often check our mailboxes hoping maybe something unexpected will come to surprise us when we least expect it. Maybe we hope against hope that some way some how there will be something quite intriguing to really make a difference in each of our days.

The following poem, "The Mystery Mailbox", is based on a true event that happened to me a few years ago. I was visiting a local beach in North Carolina and ran across a mailbox standing alone above the rushing ocean waves. As I opened this mailbox, I noticed there were all kind of letters and books that various people who walked this beach in North Carolina had left. Even though I did not get a chance to read the contents of all that was there, I could sense each one of the books and letters carried special messages of faith, hope, and love by all those who left special things behind.

If anything I realized that day that it is never too late to leave words of hope and peace to those who are reaching out for their loved ones in the most beautiful ways imaginable.

The Mystery Mailbox

I came across a picture hanging in a hotel resort
Among coastal waters far from home
It told of a story of a mystery mailbox
On an island that was standing all alone

As I read about this mailbox and the letters
From broken hearts it held inside
There was an urge within my weary spirit
To find out its secrets and why

In my quest to find this mystery mailbox
I took several walks on a comforting, sandy shore
I was convinced that God wanted me to stay determined
To learn its secrets and so much more

Then on a sunny day as I walked the beach
I saw a rusty mailbox rooted strongly in the sand
At that moment I knew I had found the key to
Life's secrets God wanted me to understand

As I opened this mailbox, I was greeted by

Letters from all sorts of curious souls
I respected their written words but could not help
But absorb the energy of their eager goals

There were tons of letters I could feel were
A cry of help for someone to soothe their minds
I looked up to Heaven and asked God to help
Them find a peaceful resolution this time

Among the letters was a book of what seemed
To be poems for the weary of heart
I realized these poetic words were strong enough
To help those in pain keep from falling apart

When I looked deeper in the mailbox I noticed
A journal of someone's lost dreams
I whispered to God and asked Him to help others
See the truth of what life really means

I took a deeper look and noticed many other notes
All wrinkled with time weary stains
It was then I prayed somehow God would help them
Know their good efforts were not in vain

As I kept staring at this mailbox
I knew sooner or later I had to leave it be
But all these writings echoed voices of
Desperation whose needs kept haunting me

Eventually I walked away from this mailbox

With its mysterious letters on my mind
I knew I had to trust God like everyone else
In this box things would work out in time

Chapter 49 - The Desperate Bridge Called Suicide

In this life we are all bombarded with challenges and disappointments that often can be too hard or too much to bear. Sometimes it seems the whole world is weighing on our shoulders, and we often seek a way out just so we don't have to feel that the walls of pain are closing in all around us. Often we just want to feel that someone somewhere understands our struggles. However, for some people, the pressures of life weigh them down so much that they feel they can't make it from one day to the next.

I know it is hard for any of us to imagine why anyone would want to take his or her own life. Even though it is hard to understand, we must put ourselves in someone else's shoes as what someone portrays on the outside may not be what he or she is really feeling on the inside. Despite the pain someone is in, we could be that person who makes a difference in someone else's life. We could be that person who could make the major difference between a life and death situation. I cannot stress enough how important it is to take another's pain to whom we feel close very seriously and to believe we could help turn around what appears to be a hopeless situation into something much more rewarding.

In the following poem, "The Desperate Bridge Called Suicide", the picture is painted of a struggling soul who is torn apart by despair and suffering, yet somehow cries out for spiritual help to give him or her the strength to want to keep on living.

The Desperate Bridge Called Suicide

I took a walk along a bridge swinging
High above the valley I call despair
Somehow I wondered if I jumped
Off the side would anyone truly care

I sat in the middle of a bridge connecting
My past and my future story
Yet the present was the problem because
I could not face life with anymore glory

As I looked back to my past, I thought of
All the times I was so misunderstood

Every time I tried to do my best someone
Put me down and left me feeling not so good

When I thought about the moments
I tried to be the hero for those in need
Somehow my spirit got lost in the wilderness
Of other people's misguided good deeds

I tried to figure out when my
Broken spirit never felt complete
All I can remember was feeling lost in a world
Where negative energy caused me much defeat

I hung my head low on this bridge
Of pain wondering what I should do
All I could see were the dark clouds of pain
Crushing my heart all the way through

I looked to the other side of the bridge
For a glimpse of my future path
All I could see was a broken heart
That was truly unable to look back

Every place I envisioned in the future
I could not figure out where to turn
The images of being hurt again felt like a strong fire
I could not escape, only left to be burned

As I took a glimpse of the future in the hope
Of trying to see something brighter

I could feel the anxiety of false hopes
And dreams make my chest feel tighter

In the present moment I knew I had the choice
To live or die to be free from it all
My emotional turmoil kept pulling me deeper
Into an abyss of sadness I could not solve

Despite my sadness, the darkened sky above me
Faded into the most peaceful sunset to calm my troubled soul
Then before me the most tranquil flock of birds flew by
As if to say embrace the wings of hope and trust God will
never let you go

Chapter 50 - True Destiny

I feel that we all have a destiny. Sometimes it is hard to understand what we are meant to do or where we are meant to go. However, I truly feel that we have each been given a unique life path, and there will be many ups and downs along the way of each of our journeys. However, through all the ups and downs, we will discover that each of us is destined for greatness.

The following poem, "True Destiny", is all about searching for one's meaning in life as he or she navigates the path of life trying to put it all in perspective.

As I have learned, the key to finding our true destiny is to never lose sight of hope as it holds the key to helping us endure those stormy times knowing great days lie ahead.

True Destiny

I fell in love with destiny because it had
Everything I needed and more
Yet somehow my confusion from misguided chances
Kept me closed behind uncertain doors

I walked around in the abyss of my heart
Wondering why life was so up and down
I realized I needed to figure out how to
Redirect my energies to a more peaceful sound

In the wilderness of too many voices
Everyone thought they knew what I needed
Yet the spiritual call of come trust in me was
All my weary spirit really heeded

From one moment to the next I thought
Driving around in my car would solve the issue
Yet every crossroad I came to was not very clear
So my tear-filled eyes kept reaching for a tissue

So I came to a roadblock trying to interfere
With what my heart completely wanted
I was tired of falling back to past hurts
That kept my soul feeling truly haunted

The negative energies of frustration tried to tell me
Nothing happened for a reason
Yet I knew in my heart that all the good and bad of this life
Came about for a destined season

As I got back into my car, I wondered how much longer
I could keep testing fate
A voice from the other side said all the pain you endure
Will for sure be worth the wait

Somehow I knew I needed not to let this world
Get the complete best of me
Yet within my struggling spirit I was not sure
How to get rid of my heartfelt misery

After driving around in circles I knew
I needed to trust my intuition
Following my heart instead of my head
Was the only way to bring my dreams to fruition

When I tuned into my heart I could feel
It wanted me to not fear taking any chances
No matter what happened I could still find
Peace of mind in the most difficult circumstances

Despite all the wrong turns I made on my trip
To try and figure out my life path
I knew trusting my heart's desires helped me
Embrace my true destiny without ever looking back

Afterword

After reading, *Embracing Hope in the Midst of Stormy Times*, it is my desire that the reflections and poetry throughout this book give you the assurance that everything in this life happens for a reason. No matter what the reasons may be, it is important that we never lose hope that a better outcome awaits us.

Remember that everything you endure has a lesson, and no matter how hard that lesson may be, it is meant for each of us to learn and understand that everything will be ok. We can't always control or change what happens to us, but we can control the ways we react to what comes our way with dignity and grace.

Throughout my own times of challenges and frustrations, I learned to hold onto hope that better days lie ahead. I would encourage each of you to remember if you can survive all the hard times that come against you, then you can face any problems you encounter.

Keep embracing hope in the midst of stormy times, and you will find a beautiful rainbow of new beginnings waiting to bring your heart and soul much needed happiness and peace.

About the Author

After writing my books, *Spiritual Whispers to the Soul*, *Living and Learning from the Healing Waters of Courage*, and *Magical Love Messages Between Kindred Spirits*, I felt led to write a book that is all about the beauty of having hope.

Embracing Hope in the Midst of Stormy Times reflects the true realities of this life. It would be wonderful if the highs of life could always be in existence. However, the truth is life is always going to have tough moments and times of suffering. Therefore, we each must learn to hang on to hope even when it seems all of life's odds are against us.

My goal is to continue to write more books under my publishing name, Colorful Spirit Publishing, so I can always help others find their truth and appreciate a more fulfilling way of life. For more information on where to find all my books, please visit my website at www.colorfulspirit.com or feel free to email me at hwright@colorfulspirit.com. You can also find many of my individual writings for sale at my online store at www.colorfulspirit.gifts.

Always remember to hold on to hope and trust that everything has a way of working our for the best!

Sincerely,
Heather D. Wright

www.ingramcontent.com/pod-product-compliance
Lightning Source LLC
Chambersburg PA
CBHW031621040426
42452CB00007B/606